I SEE NOTHING BUT THE HORRORS OF A CIVIL WAR
Second Edition

Alexander R. Cain

Title:	I See Nothing But the Horrors of a Civil War (Second Edition)
ID:	15041599
Category:	History
Copyright Year:	© 2019
ISBN:	9781090942036

To My Children, John and Abigail.
Thank You for All the Laughs and Wonderful Times

TABLE OF CONTENTS

Our Country is lost in dissipation, luxury and faction. There is no publick Spirit or virtue left either to reward merrit or punish offences. Remove all Such wretches from power and leav either Execution of affairs to the brave, zealous Loyalists, who have lost their fortunes and Risk'd their lives in defence of their King and Country; such are the men who will save their Country from Ruin and distruction...

~John Hamilton

Chapter One: Introduction

It is commonly stated that history is written by the victor and the American Revolution is no exception. As a result of the rebel triumph at the conclusion the War for Independence, those who remained faithful to the crown have often been depicted in a negative light. In countless historical works, legal documents and even in popular culture, loyalists were typically portrayed as a corrupt, inept and greedy people whose blind devotion to the British crown led to their downfall.[1] However, such a glaring and erroneous stereotype only trivialized the struggles that the American loyalist endured during the War for Independence.

By the conclusion of the American Revolution, between 80,000 and 100,000 loyalists had fled the American colonies. Almost half of them escaped to Canada. Of those, 45,000 refugees settled in the

---

[1] A modern example is the film *The Patriot.* In that film, loyalist soldiers are portrayed as power hungry individuals who have no reservation in committing war crimes against the American populace.

Canadian Maritime region. An additional 9,500 refugees fled to the Quebec Province. Of those, approximately 7,500 ultimately settled in Upper Canada. These men, women and children left behind more than their homes. They left behind their experiences, communities, friends and relatives, businesses and personal belongings.[2]

Many colonists who ultimately became "Tories" were not distinguishable from their neighbors who embraced independence. Many loyalists were respected members of their towns; they were often well-educated Harvard graduates who worked as merchants, doctors, lawyers, distillers or ministers. Individuals such as Sir John Johnson, Richard Saltonstall, Jonathan Sewell and Admiralty Judge Samuel Curwen, who would later enlist in the loyalist cause, were seen prior to the American Revolution as leading and influential members of their respective colonies. However, most colonists from New York and New England who remained faithful to the crown hailed from the middle and lower classes of the American colonies. These loyalists enjoyed neither wealth nor privilege.

---

[2] Bruce Wilson, *As She Began: An Illustrated Introduction to Loyalist Ontario*, (Toronto: Dundurn Group, 1981), 13.

Of the four hundred eighty-eight loyalists who eventually settled in the Ontario region of Upper Canada following the American Revolution and submitted claims to the British government for losses sustained during the war, only five held public office. Three of those were considered modest political posts. Only one claimant, a physician, would be considered a professional by modern standards. A small number owned shops, ran taverns or were considered artisans. Ninety percent of those loyalists who settled in the Ontario region simply identified themselves as farmers.[3]

In 2016, historian Amber Jolly examined the court records of over eight hundred and fifty loyalist property seizure cases in New York following the passage of the Confiscation Act of 1783.[4] According to her research, the overwhelming majority of loyalists who lost property in New York were from the laboring, agricultural and artisan classes. For example, court records assert that almost four hundred loyalists were listed as yeomen, two hundred were identified as farmers, and an additional

---

[3] Ibid.

[4] According to Jolly, the largest number of property confiscations occurred in Albany and Tryon Counties.

sixty four were simply listed as "laborers". Nineteen men were listed as

blacksmiths, seventeen as tailors, sixteen as carpenters and six as

shoemakers. Other loyalist occupations identified by Jolly included

wheelrights, saddlers, marriners, bakers, coopers, ship wrights and hatters.

Four pieces of confiscated property were owned by single loyalist women,

while an additional two were seized from widows. Only six percent were

considered "professional" by modern standards.[5]

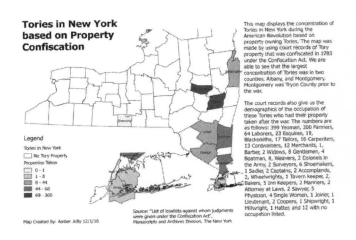

Tories in New York based on Property Confiscation

This map displays the concentration of Tories in New York during the American Revolution based on property owning Tories. The map was made by using court records of Tory property that was confiscated in 1783 under the Confiscation Act. We are able to see that the largest concentration of Tories was in two counties, Albany, and Montgomery. Montgomery was Tryon County prior to the war.

The court records also give us the demographics of the occupation of these Tories who had their property taken after the war. The numbers are as follows: 399 Yeoman, 200 Farmers, 64 Laborers, 23 Esquires, 19, Blacksmiths, 17 Tailors, 16 Carpenters, 13 Cordwainers, 12 Merchants, 1, Barber, 2 Widows, 8 Gentlemen, 4 Boatman, 8, Weavers, 2 Colonels in the Army, 2 Surveyors, 6 Shoemakers, 1 Sadler, 2 Captains, 2 Accomplands, 2, Wheelwrights, 1 Tavern keeper, 2, Bakers, 5 Inn Keepers, 2 Mariners, 2 Attorney at Laws, 2 Sawyer, 5 Physician, 4 Single Women, 1 Joiner, 1 Lieutenant, 2 Coopers, 1 Shipwright, 1 Millwright, 1 Hatter; and 12 with no occupation listed.

Legend
Tories in New York
No Tory Property
Properties Taken
0 - 1
1 - 8
9 - 44
44 - 68
68 - 300

Source: "List of loyalists against whom judgments were given under the Confiscation Act", Manuscripts and Archives Division, The New York

Map Created By: Amber Jolly 12/1/16

---

[5] Amber Jolly, *Tories in New York Based Upon Property Confiscation* (December 1, 2016); *List of Loyalists Against Whom Judgements were Given Under the Confiscation Act"*, Manuscripts and Archive Division, The New York Public Library. Only twenty three men were identified by Jolly as "esquires". An additional eight men were labeled as gentlemen while twelve were listed as merchants. Seven men had occupations that were identified as physicians or attorneys. Only four were military officers.

The average loyalist farmer who ultimately took refuge in Upper Canada leased or owned less than two hundred acres of land prior to the American Revolution. Forty-two percent of the Ontario settlers admitted they had cleared less than ten acres of land prior to their flight.[6] Fifty-four percent of the farmers hailed from Tyron County, New York. An additional twenty-five percent had ties to Albany County. Fourteen percent claimed Charlotte County as their prior residence.[7]

Over half of the refugees who settled in Upper Canada were foreign born. Over fifty percent of Ontario loyalists were Scot Highland Roman Catholics. Second in number were German and Irish immigrants. An additional eight percent claimed England as their place of birth. At the start of the American Revolution, many loyalist Scot immigrants had only resided in the American colonies for four years. English immigrants had resided in America on average for eight years. By comparison, many Irish

---

[6] Ibid.
[7] Ibid.

and German immigrants had lived in the colonies between eleven and eighteen years.[8]

Joining these loyalists were African-American loyalists. Almost ten percent of loyalists who fled to Canada were of African-American descent. Whether slave or freeman, many African-Americans cast their lot with the crown in an attempt to secure a better life for themselves and their families. Likewise, many Native American allies of the crown also retreated to Canada after the war. Over two thousand Iroquois from the Six Nations, Mohicans, Nanticokes and Squakis had settled in the Ontario region by 1785.[9]

Regardless of their economic or social background, native born whites, immigrants, slaves, freemen and Native Americans banded together in support of King George and the British government. Regardless of the lack of supplies, political support or financial backing, the campaign to defend the British crown was enthusiastically and

---

[8] Ibid.
[9] Ibid, 10.

admirably waged by loyalists from the print of local newspapers to the siege lines of Yorktown. Granted, their defense of British policy often fell on deaf ears and their military endeavors were often insufficient to turn the tide of war. However, their willingness to undertake such endeavors is noteworthy.

This is the story of the men, women and children from New York and the Hampshire Grants who chose to remain faithful to the Crown and fought as part of McAlpin's Corps of American Volunteers.

Chapter Two: "The Purest Principles of Loyalty"

Despite popular belief most loyalists did not support the crown out of blind loyalty or a misguided sense of patriotism. Instead, most chose to remain loyal due to a variety of personal, societal and religious principles. For some, religious teachings demanded loyalty to the Crown. For others, economic opportunity guided fealty to King George. For more than a few, cultural beliefs dictated support of the British government. Yet regardless of their respective motivations, the American loyalists found themselves quickly at odds with their "patriot" counterparts.

One guiding principle which influenced Tories to remain loyal to the Crown was religious beliefs. Regardless of religious affiliation, many loyalists adhered to religious teachings and interpretations of the bible that required solemn allegiance to the Crown. For Anglicans, many ministers firmly believed they were bound by oath to be loyal to the king. The

16

Reverend Benjamin Pickman insisted he had to remain loyal out of the "purest Principles of Loyalty to my late Sovereign".[10] Fellow Anglican John Amory refused to support the American cause because "I could not with a quiet conscience...take an Oath that I would bear Arms against the King of Great Britain to whom I had already sworn Allegiance."[11]

Not all Congregationalists supported the revolutionary rhetoric that was frequently espoused from the pulpit in New England. Isaac Smith justified his loyalty to the crown upon religious principles. He publicly argued that his position at Harvard and his profession as a Congregational minister forbade him to be disobedient to his king or Parliament, because they obliged him to "liberal enquiry."[12] As Smith declared in a letter to his cousin Mary Smith Cranch, his unwavering devotion to the crown was

---

[10] Benjamin Pickman. *Benjamin Pickman to his wife*, February 20, 1783, Letter, Benjamin Pickman Correspondence, Essex Institute, Salem, Massachusetts.

[11] John Armory. *John Amory to James Lovell, Providence*, February 12, 1778, Letter, quoted Zoltan Haraszti, "A Loyalist in spite of himself," *More books*, Vol. 22, No. 9 (Boston: 1947), 338-339.

[12] Isaac Smith, *Isaac Smith Jr. to Mary Smith Cranch*, Cambridge, October 20, 1774, and *Mary Smith Cranch to Isaac Smith Jr.,* Boston, October 15, 1774, Adams Family Correspondence, II. Series, Vols. 1, ed. by H. Butterfield, Marc Friedlaender, (Cambridge: 1963).

preferable to being "subject to the capricious, unlimited despotism" of his "own countrymen."[13]

Sandemanians, a pacifist sect of Congregationalists, also believed that the bible commanded absolute loyalty to the Crown. Samuel Pike, a prominent Sandemanian, personified this belief when he declared in 1766 that every Christian must be a loyal subject to civil authority, even if that ruler was tyrannical. In turn, many became outspoken critics of the American cause and quickly became embroiled in the political crisis of the 1760s and early 1770s. The Sandemanians were the first to brand the Sons of Liberty and other political organizations as traitors to the Crown. One sect member, Colburn Barrell, declared that the Boston Massacre was the direct result of treasonous Congregationalist ministers who defied the laws of the land.

Roman Catholics, often seen as the scourge of the British Empire, quickly found themselves being forced to side with the Crown. With the passage of the Quebec Act of 1774, the practice of the Catholic faith was

---

[13] Ibid.

18

no longer subject to restrictions in certain regions of North America. The concept of Roman Catholics openly practicing their religious beliefs in New York and New England deeply concerned their Congregationalist and Anglican neighbors. Members of the New York Provincial Congress quickly warned, "the indulgence and establishment of Popery all along the interior confines of the Protestant Colonies tends not only to obstruct their growth, but to weaken their security."[14]

Yet religious principles were not the only motivating factor to remain loyal to the crown. Often, economic dependency and patronage dictated one's loyalty. Political appointees like William Woolton, Thomas Hutchinson and Andrew Oliver naturally sided with the British government because their respective colonial posts ensured potential profit. For many merchants, siding with the rebel mobs almost guaranteed financial ruin. Joseph Hooper, also known as "King Hooper", of

---

[14] "Motion by Mr. Melancton Smith, for an addition to the Report for securing the liberty of conscience, read, amended, and adopted, Motion by Mr. McDougall, that the Plan of Accommodation be not transmitted to the Congress until called for by them, or by our Delegates there." New York Congress, June 24, 1775. From *American Archives* Series 4, Volume 2, Page 1317.

Marblehead was heavily dependent on trade with England. John Amory feared economic loss if he ended his business relationships with England. Amory was among the merchants who protested against the "Solemn League and Covenant of 1774," which called for the suspending of all commercial business with Great Britain. A business trip to England, which he coincidentally made during the Battle of Lexington, branded him a "Tory" in the eyes of his countrymen.

However, loyalty to the Crown in the name of economic preservation was not limited to wealthy businessmen. Many tenant farmers of Albany, Ulster and Tryon Counties in New York colony were heavily dependent upon their loyalist landlords for continued economic success. In other words, if rebel policies and practices drove their masters to financial ruin, economic destruction would surely follow for the tenants as well.

Likewise, economic opportunity in the form of recruitment bounties attracted many to the loyalist cause as the War for Independence progressed. Financial incentives were offered to prospective recruits, however, more important was the promise of freehold land. As early as 1775 recruiters for the Royal Highland Emigrants, a corps of loyalist Scot Highlanders, promised 200 acres of land to prospective soldiers. Ebenezer Jessup, lieutenant-colonel of the King's Loyal Americans and a large landowner, pledged 24,000 acres of his land to those who "would serve faithfully during the War ... and 20,000 more to such of my officers as shuld merit the same by their good conduct."[15] Recruiters in Bergen County, New Jersey, were even more generous, promising 200 acres of land for each adult male, 100 acres for his wife, and fifty acres for each child. In March 1777 the governor of Quebec promised loyalists who "shall continue to serve His Majesty until the rebellion is suppressed and peace restored ... [a] bounty of 200 acres of land." In May 1781, when recruiting was more difficult, recruits were promised the same land after only three years of service and were given six guineas for enlisting.

---

[15] Alexander McDonell. *Alexander McDonell to General Howe, October 30, 1775.* Letter; Lord George Germain. *Germain to Carleton, March 26, 1777.* Letter; Guy Carleton. *Carleton to Butler, May 18, 1777.* Letter; Ebenezer Jessup. *Ebenezer Jessup to Burgoyne, July 17, 1778.* Letter.

A desire for public safety and order also influenced many colonists who remained loyal to the Crown. Looking back at the origins of the American Revolution, key players such as Jonathan Sewall viewed the original conflict not with the Stamp Act Crisis or the attempt by the British government to collect on its debt from the French Wars. Instead, many loyalists saw the Writ of Assistance case as the ignition of conflict. To many loyal to the Crown, the Writ of Assistance case was viewed as an attempt by ambitious politicians to overthrow the political establishment and replace it with a lawless or populist mob. Thus, most loyalists detested the mob rule that spread from Boston and New York City to the countryside and abhorred the lack of order. As tensions grew between the colonies and England, many colonists attempted to remain neutral. However, as radicals seized power, neutrality became impossible. Dr. William Paine gave up his neutrality and declared himself a loyalist after he experienced "too many abuses" and "insults" from Patriots. Anglican minister William Walter shuddered at the deprivation of English rights and warned "I see nothing But the horrors of a Civil War."[16] Samuel Curwen,

Judge of Admiralty, complained Whig "tempers get more and more soured

and malevolent against all moderate men, whom they see fit to reproach as

enemies of their country by the name of Tories, among whom I am

unhappily (although unjustly) ranked."[17] The Reverend Samuel Seabury

of Westchester, New York, lashed out at the patriot mobs who routinely

and illegally entered and searched loyalist homes:

> Do as you please: If you like it better, choose your
> Committee, or suffer it to be Chosen by half a dozen Fools
> in your neighborhood – open your doors to them let them
> examine your tea canisters, and molasses-jugs, and your
> wives and daughters pettycoats – bow and cringe and
> tremble and quake – fall down and worship our sovereign
> Lord the Mob . . . and shall my house be entered into and
> my mode of living enquired into, by a domineering

---

[16] *William Clark to Joseph Pattern*, Boston, August 6 1774, and *to M. Fisher*, Boston, August 6, 1774, William Clark Papers, Diocesan Library, Boston, Massachusetts.
[17] Samuel Curwen. *Journal and Letters of the Late Samuel Curwen, Judge of Admiralty, etc., an American refugee in England from 1775-1784, Comprising Remarks on the Prominent Men and Measures of that Period: To Which are Added Biographical Notices of Many American Loyalists, and Other Eminent Persons, May 4, 1775.* Journal. From California Digital Library. https://archive.org/details/curwensamuelj00curwrich.

Committee-man? Before I submit I will die, live you and be slaves.[18]

For many loyalists in the New York region, especially those of Scottish descent, loyalty to the Crown was determined by cultural beliefs. Following the conclusion of the French and Indian War, many Scottish veterans from the 42nd, 77th, and 78th Regiments settled in the Albany area. In a society where clan ties were often paramount, many Scottish residents in the Albany area viewed King George III as their Laird or clan chieftain.[19] As a result, most refused to sign "association" documents or loyalty oaths put forth by New York Tory Committees due to the fact such documents were viewed as breaking an oath of allegiance to the King.[20] As Captain Alexander McDonald, formerly of the 77th Regiment, warned "I am determined to be true to the trust reposed in me and discharge my

---

[18] Seabury, Samuel. *Free Thoughts on the Proceedings of the Continental Congress, 1774*. Pamphlet. From Project Canterbury.
http://anglicanhistory.org/usa/seabury/farmer/.
[19] J. Fraser, *Skulking for the King*, (Ontario: Boston Mills Press, 1985), 12-13.
[20] Ibid,13.

duty with honour . . . as long as I live." [21]

Finally, for those colonists who attempted to remain neutral or initially sided with the "patriot" cause, the Declaration of Independence instead drove many individuals over to the side of the Crown. Seen as either a radical document or an extreme reaction to the dispute with the Crown, men such as Justus Sherwood, renounced their affiliation with the American cause and took up arms for the King.

---

[21] Ibid,11.

Chapter Three: The Conflict Ignites

Following its conquest of Canada during the French and Indian War, England began to recognize the harsh realities of its victory. In the months after the Treaty of Paris in 1763, Great Britain was forced to not only administer its newly acquired territories, but also to defend them. This necessitated maintaining a ten thousand-man army to protect North America from future French operations and Native American attacks, such as Pontiac's Rebellion, which ignited after the conclusion of the war. By January 5, 1763, Britain's funded debt was a staggering £122,603,336 with an annual interest of £4,409,797. A year later, the debt was almost £7,000,000 larger and by January of 1767, it had increased yet another £7,000,000.[22]

In an attempt to curb this financial crisis, the British government

---

[22] Robert Middlekauf, *The Glorious Cause: The American Revolution, 1763 - 1789*, (New York: Oxford University Press, 1982), 57.

implemented a series of economic programs aimed at having those it considered to have benefited most by the successful conclusion of the war, the American colonies, share in the burden of debt. After reviewing the state of Britain's finances, Chancellor of Exchequer, George Grenville, concluded that the American colonies had benefited greatly from the protection of the Crown while contributing very little in taxes. At the same time, Grenville pointed out, an active smuggling trade coupled with massive colonial customs mismanagement, particularly in the New England region, had led to an annual £6,000 deficit in custom duties collected in American ports. Accordingly, he suggested that a direct tax be levied on the American colonies in order to generate additional revenue.[23]

The first two revenue raising measures that Great Britain imposed on her American colonies were the Sugar Act of 1764 and the Stamp Act of 1765. The Sugar Act established tariffs on colonial trading and also attempted to curb the American practice of smuggling sugar and molasses

---

[23] Grenville also established reforms in the way custom duties were collected and accounted.

from the West Indies by placing a three pence per gallon tax on foreign

molasses. The act established a list of "enumerated goods" that could only

be shipped to England and set forth procedures for the accounting, loading

and unloading of cargo in port. Violations of the act were prosecuted in a

vice admiralty court, where defendants would be denied the right to a jury

trial and where the presumption was of guilt rather than innocence. The

second revenue raising measure was the Stamp Act, which levied an

unprecedented direct tax on almost every piece of public paper in the

colonies. Newspapers, almanacs, deeds, wills, custom documents, even

playing cards were among the many papers subjected to the tax. The

Stamp Act went so far as to impose a tax upon *tax receipts*.

The Sugar and Stamp acts brought on an explosion of riots,

boycotts and protests throughout the colonies, particularly in

Massachusetts and New York. At first, Massachusetts' response was

peaceful, with the inhabitants merely boycotting certain goods. However,

resistance to the taxes soon became more violent. Under the guidance of

Samuel Adams, Bostonians began a campaign of terror directed against those who supported the Stamp Act. It began on August 14, 1765 with an effigy of Andrew Oliver, the appointed stamp distributor for Massachusetts, being hung from a "liberty tree" in plain view by the "sons of liberty." That evening, the luxurious Oliver home was burned to the ground. A chastened Oliver quickly resigned his commission. The following evening, incited by a rumor that he supported the Stamp Act, the home of Thomas Hutchinson, Lieutenant Governor of the colony, was surrounded by an unruly mob. When Hutchinson refused to accede to the demand that he come out and explain his position, the mob broke several windows and then dispersed. Two weeks later, on August 28, 1765, an even larger mob assembled and descended upon the homes of several individuals suspected of favoring the Stamp Act, including again that of the Lieutenant Governor. Hutchinson managed to evacuate his family to safety before the mob arrived. Then, as Hutchinson later described it, "the hellish crew fell upon my house with the rage of divels and in a moment with axes split down the door and entered. My son heard them cry 'damn him he is upstairs we'll have him.' Some ran immediately as high as the top of the house, others filled the rooms below and cellars and others remained without the house to be employed there. I was obliged to retire thro yards and gardens to a house more remote where I remained until 4 o'clock by which time one of the best finished houses in the Province had nothing remaining but the bare walls and floors."[24]

18th Century image of loyalist abuse. Artist Unknown.

The mob's show of force had the desired effect. With Oliver's

[24] Thomas Hutchinson. *Hutchinson to Richard Jackson, August 30, 1765.* Letter. From Hutchinson Correspondence, Massachusetts Archives (microfilm), vol. 26, 146-147.

resignation, the stamps could not be properly distributed. Additionally, no other stamp officer was willing to step forward to assume Oliver's legal role. In short, Boston was crippled and could not enforce the act. The town standoff between Boston and the Crown continued through the fall and winter of 1765.

Meanwhile, in New York City a meeting of the merchants of the city was called at Burns's Coffee House on Broadway to address passage of the Stamp Act. As a result of the gathering, a non-importation agreement was signed. The following day, November 1, 1765, two companies of the Sons of Liberty appeared on the streets. According to John Holt

> The matter was intended to be done privately, but it got wind, and by ten O'Clock I suppose 2000 people attended at the Coffee House, among them most of the principal men in town . . . Two men were dispatched to the Collector for the Stamped Bonds of which he had 30 in all, he desired Liberty to confer with the Governor, which was granted. The Governor sent Word, if the Stamps were delivered to him, he would give his word and honor they should not be used; but if people were not satisfied with this, they might do as they pleased with them – The message being returned to the gathering multitude, they would not agree to the Governors proposal, but insist upon the Stamps being delivered and burned, one or two men attended by about a thousand others

were then sent for the Stamps, which were brought to the Coffee House, and the Merchant who had used them was ordered himself to kindle the fire and consume them, those filed in and all, this was accordingly done amidst the Huzza's of the people who were by this time swelled to the Number one supposes of about 5000, and in another hour I suppose would have been 10,000 – The people pretty quietly dispersed soon After, but their Resentment was not allayed . . .[25]

One company marched to the Commons where they hanged in effigy Lieutenant-Governor Cadwallader Colden; the other company broke into Colden's stable and took out his chariot, in which they "placed a copy of the obnoxious act and an effigy of the lieutenant-governor." Both companies then united and marched in silence to the Bowling Green, where they found soldiers drawn up on the ramparts of a nearby fortification ready to receive them. General Gage, the British commander, thought it prudent "not to fire upon the rioters; and, as they were refused admission to the fort, they turned their attention to the wooden railing

---

[25] John Holt. *John Holt to Mrs. Deborah Franklin, February 15, 1766.* Letter.

which surrounded the little park. This they tore down for fuel; and, having

burnt railing, carriage, act, and effigy, they dispersed to their homes."[26]

The Bostonians in Distress by Phillip Dawe, 1774

With the riots receiving widespread coverage in London

newspapers coupled with the successful boycott program undertaken by

---

[26] Ibid. "Toward the Evening . . . tho' the Sons of Liberty exerted themselves to the utmost, they could not prevent the gathering of the Multitude, who went to Mr. Williams's house, broke open the Door and destroyed some of the Furniture. . . The people were generally satisfied and soon dispersed--but many of those of inferior Sort, who delight in mischief merely for its own sake, or for plunder, seem yet to be in such a turbulent Disposition that the two mortified Gentlemen are still in some Danger, but the Sons of Liberty intend to Exert themselves in their Defense."

New York, Philadelphia and Boston, England finally yielded. Realizing the Stamp and Sugar Acts could never be enforced in America, the acts were repealed on March 4, 1766. However, before striking the laws, Parliament announced the Declaratory Act of 1766, which emphasized its authority to legislate for the colonies in all cases whatsoever.

It was not long before the members of the Parliament made use of the principle expressed in the Declaratory Act. In 1767, England faced a projected annual cost of almost £400,000 to maintain her army in America. Charles Townshend, the impetuous Chancellor of the Exchequer, of whom it was said, "his mouth often outran his mind", suddenly announced that he knew how to tax the American colonies. To meet this crisis, Townshend suggested, and Parliament enacted, a series of laws directed at raising revenue from the American colonies. The Townshend Acts, as they became known, provided for an American import tax on paper, painter's lead, glass and tea. The acts also tightened custom policies and revived the vice-admiralty courts. Although a minority within the House of Commons opposed such a measure, the majority rationalized it would "raise colonial revenue, punish the colonists for their ill-behavior after the repeal of the Stamp Act, and exercise the rights to which Parliament laid claim in the Declaratory Act." The House of Commons was so pleased with its role in the venture that it promptly voted to lower English land taxes from four shillings on the pound to three, resulting in a £500,000 loss of revenue and threatening fiscal chaos.

Boston stood at the forefront of opposition and by 1768, Boston was once again resorting to violence to indicate its opposition to British policy. In March, rioters went to "Commissioner Burch's home and with clubs assembled before his door a great part of the evening, and he was obliged to send away his wife and children by a back door."[27] Inspector William Woolton returned home one evening to find "4 men passing him, one with a stick or bludgeon in his hand accosted him saying, 'Damn your Blood we will be at you to morrow night."[28] The victims of the mob begged Governor Bernard to apply for military protection so the

---

[27] Francis Bernard. *Bernard to Earl of Shelburne, March 19, 1768.* Letter. From Bernard Papers, v. 11, 191-193.
[28] Deposition of William Woolton, March 18, 1768.

Townshend Acts could be enforced. The governor struggled with the decision, but ultimately applied to the king for troops. At the same time, however, British merchants pleaded with Parliament and the King to repeal the act before they were brought to financial ruin. Unfortunately their pleas went unanswered. In 1768, Governor Bernard was ordered to dissolve the Massachusetts legislature, and two full regiments of British regulars were dispatched to Boston to protect the custom officials and help to enforce the Townshend Acts.

New York took a more cautious approach in response to the Townshend Acts and instead implemented a widespread boycott of goods. Specifically, on September 5, 1768, New York City merchants and tradesmen resolved

> Reflecting on the salutary [beneficial/curative] Measures entered into by the People of *Boston* and this City to restrict the Importation of Goods from Great Britain until the Acts of Parliament laying Duties on Paper, Glass, &c. were repealed; and being animated with a Spirit of Liberty and thinking it our Duty to exert ourselves by all lawful Means to maintain and obtain our just Rights and Privileges, which we claim under our most excellent Constitution as Englishmen, not to be taxed but by our own Consent or that of our Representatives; and in order to support and

strengthen our Neighbors, the Merchants of this City, we the Subscribers [signers], uniting in the common Cause, do agree to and with each other, as follows:

First, That we will not ourselves purchase or take any Goods or Merchandise imported from Europe by any Merchant directly or indirectly, contrary to the true Intent and Meaning of an Agreement of the Merchants of this City, on the twenty-seventh of August last.

Secondly, That we will not ourselves, or by any other Means, buy any Kind of Goods from any Merchant, Storekeeper, or Retailer (if any such there be) who shall refuse to join with their Brethren in signing the said Agreement; but that we will use every lawful Means in our Power to prevent our Acquaintance from dealing with them.

Thirdly, That if any Merchant, in or from Europe, should import any Goods in order to sell them in this Province contrary to the above Agreement, that we ourselves will by no Means deal with such Importers; and as far as we can, by all lawful Means, endeavor to discourage the Sale of such Goods.

Fourthly, That we will endeavor to fall upon some Expedient to make known such Importers or Retailers as shall refuse to unite in maintaining and obtaining the Liberties of their Country.

Fifthly, That we, his Majesty's most dutiful and loyal Subjects, Inhabitants of the City of New York, being filled with Love and Gratitude to our present most gracious Sovereign, and the highest Veneration for the British Constitution, which we unite to plead as our Birth Right; and are always willing to unite to support and maintain, give it as our Opinion, and are determined to deem that Persons who shall refuse to unite in the Common Cause, as acting the Part of an Enemy to the true Interest of Great Britain and her Colonies, and consequently not deserving the Patronage of Merchants or Mechanics.[29]

However, as a direct result of the boycott New York sunk into an economic depression and tensions continued to rise between colonists and the British government. On January 19, 1770, New York merchant Isaac Sears and others attempted to stop a group of British soldiers from passing out handbills criticizing local citizens. The pamphlets chastised the local citizenry over a failed attempt by regulars to destroy a liberty pole erected on Golden Hill in New York City. Sears detained some of the soldiers and marched his captives towards the mayor's office, while the rest of the British regulars retreated to their barracks to sound the alarm.

A crowd of townsfolk soon arrived but were confronted by a score of soldiers. "In the mean Time, a considerable Number of People collected opposite to the Mayor's. Shortly after, about twenty Soldiers with Cutlasses and Bayonets from the lower Barracks made their

---

[29] "Tradesmen's Resolves, September 5, 1768". From National Humanities Center. http://nationalhumanitiescenter.org/pds/makingrev/crisis/text4/townshendactsresponse1767.pdf

Appearance"[30] The soldiers, who were greatly outnumbered, were quickly

surrounded.   Nevertheless, they attempted to rescue their companions

who were held captive in the mayor's office. "When the Soldiers came

opposite to his House, they halted. Many of them drew their Swords and

Bayonets; some say they all drew. But all that were present agree that

many did, and faced about to the Door and demanded the Soldiers in

Custody. Some of them attempted to get into the House to rescue them.

Capt. Richardson and others at the Door prevented them, and desired them

to put up their Arms and go to their Barracks, that the Soldiers were before

the Mayor who would do them Justice. The Soldiers within likewise

desired them to go away to their Barracks and leave them to the

Determination of the Mayor."[31]

Upon seeing the soldiers draw their weapons, the townsmen

quickly retreated and armed themselves. Despite attempts by local

officials and officers to defuse the situation, a full scale brawl, later called

---

[30] *The New York Gazette*, February 5, 1770. From National Humanities Center.
http://nationalhumanitiescenter.org/pds/makingrev/crisis/text5/goldenhillseidermassacre.
pdf
[31] Ibid.

the "Battle of Golden Hill", broke out. By the end of the fight, several of the soldiers were badly bruised while one "soldier received a bad cut on the shoulder."[32] One citizen was wounded in the face and had two of his teeth broken by a "stroke of a bayonet".[33] Another was stabbed and later died of his wounds.[34]

Back in Boston, on March 5, 1770, tensions spilled over into violence. As loyalist James Chalmers later noted "March 5, 1770 is a day when the rebellious citizens of the Boston Colony demonstrated their commitment to mob violence, and their willingness to be led down the path to destruction by a few evil men . . . Soldiers, at their duty posts, minding their own business and acting non-confrontational, were verbally assaulted by Bostonian men with epitaphs of 'bloody back', 'lousy rascal', 'dammed rascally scoundrel', and 'lobster son of a b----'. Physical violence was done to the soldiers, unprovoked, by the mob pelting the soldiers with snowballs, icicles, and pieces of wood . . . It is clear to us

---

[32] Ibid.
[33] Ibid.
[34] Ibid.

that this whole series of events could have been prevented if the small band of inciters did not lure the unsuspecting civilians to perform the aggressive acts perpetrated."[35] That evening, Bostonians began to badger and taunt a lone British sentry on guard duty in front of the Royal Custom House. When the crowd began to pelt him with snowballs and ice, he called for help and was reinforced by a squad of soldiers from the 29th Regiment of Foot. When the crowd pressed closer, the nervous regulars opened fire. Five men in the crowd were killed and a number of others were wounded.

The soldiers were arrested, tried and all but two were acquitted.[36] The Boston Massacre, as the incident became known, sparked widespread outrage and pushed the colonies dangerously close to rebellion. To forestall an uprising, Parliament again retreated, repealing all the Townshend Acts, except a symbolic tax on tea of which no immediate

---

[35] https://www.americanrevolution.org/loyalist5.php
[36] Two soldiers were found guilty of manslaughter, branded on their thumbs and then released.

attempt was made to collect.[37]

However, in 1773, Parliament passed the Tea Act in an effort to finally collect the tax on tea, and to refinance the shaky economic base of the British East India Company. Established in 1709, the East India Company derived over ninety-percent of its profits from the sale of tea. By 1772, due to severe mismanagement, the company was in desperate need of a bailout. The company directors looked to Parliament for relief. Parliament's response was the Tea Act, through which the East India Company was given exclusive rights to ship tea to America without paying import duties and to sell it through their agents to American retailers. American merchants who had for years purchased tea from non-British sources (Dutch tea was a particular favorite of New Englanders) faced the prospect of financial ruin.

Massachusetts immediately opposed the act and began to organize a resistance movement. On November 29, 1773, the tea ship *Dartmouth*

---

[37] For the next two years, tensions seemed to lessen in the colonies, particularly Massachusetts. However, when Parliament attempted to control provincial judges in 1772 by directly controlling their salaries, Massachusetts quickly responded in opposition and protest.

arrived at Griffin's Wharf in Boston. Three days later, the *Beaver* and the *Eleanor* arrived at the same wharf. Bostonians demanded that Governor Hutchinson order the three ships back to England. On December 16, 1773, the owner of the *Dartmouth* apparently agreed and went to Hutchinson to beg him to let the ships return to England. Hutchinson refused, and at approximately six o'clock that evening, some 150 men and boys disguised as Indians marched to the three ships, boarded them and dumped 340 chests of tea into Boston Harbor.

The actions of the Boston Tea Party reflected the general political mood throughout the American colonies on the eve of the revolution. Many colonists believed a set of corrupt and mysterious men had been able to assert control over George the Third, his ministers and his favorites through bribery and deceit. Most Americans were certain that powerful men were plotting to make the colonists slaves by curtailing their liberties as Englishmen.

The common belief emerged that an immoral British government, having exhausted opportunities for plunder and profit in England and

Ireland, was now seeking a dispute with the American colonies as an excuse to enslave and deprive them of their wealth and liberties. Parliament had hoped to accomplish this goal quietly, but the furor aroused in the colonies by England's economic policies had given the government a temporary setback. Now, these mysterious men, who controlled Parliament and the king's ministers, were undertaking to openly incite a war, declare Americans to be rebels and enslave them.

Colonists concerns and fears of enslavement appeared repeatedly in letters, journals, and diaries of the period following the Boston Tea Party. Of course, such colonial behavior was viewed in England as an offensive act of defiance that could not be ignored. As a result, the English Parliament adopted several harsh and restrictive measures aimed at punishing Massachusetts, particularly Boston. On March 31, 1774, King George the Third signed the Boston Port Bill, intended to severely reprimand rebellious Boston. The port was closed to all seagoing traffic until damages for the destroyed tea were paid in full. The Massachusetts Provincial Charter of 1691, which residents viewed as a sacred guarantee of their liberties, was revoked. Additional regiments of regulars were dispatched to Boston and Major General Thomas Gage replaced Thomas Hutchinson as governor. Gage moved the seat of government from Boston to Salem and the customs office from Boston to Plymouth. The Governor's Council was replaced with a non-elective Mandamus Council, town meetings were prohibited without the consent of the governor and jury trials were abolished.

Any hope of avoiding a civil war now seemed dashed. In Boston, Hugh Earl Percy correctly surmised the state of affairs in the colonies on the eve of the American Revolution. "Things here are now drawing to a crisis every day. The people here openly oppose the New Acts. They have taken up arms . . . & have drove in the Gov't & most of the Council . . . In short, this country is now in an open state of rebellion."[38]

By 1775, the seeds of rebellion had seeped into New York's Albany County. Although initially slow to respond, many Albany County

---

[38] Hugh Earl Percy. *Percy to the Duke of Northumberland, September 12, 1774.* Letter.

residents ultimately turned against their Tory neighbors.[39] Armed night watches roamed the streets of Albany, the county seat, in an attempt to intimidate those loyal to the King and English government.[40] Organized "committees" disrupted meetings held in Albany's town hall between the Tory leaning mayor and his aldermen. Local businessmen with questionable loyalties, including the prominent Richard Cartwright, were

---

[39] In a 1774 letter from Thomas Young to John Lamb, Young lamented the slow response of the Colony of New York as compared to Massachusetts.

[40] "Resolved. That Mess- Abraham Cuyler and Hendrick Wendell be a Committee to apply to Mr Dirck Ten Broeck for two hundred Stand of small Arms of the Parcel he is Possessed of, and when they are procured to put such of them as require it in proper Hands to be prepared and made fit for immediate Service. From the present state and Turbulance of the County from the Alarm arisen by Suspicion of the Negroes — From the information of Col. Johnson respecting the Canadians and on Account of the great uneasiness of the Inhabitants, on these Occasions We conceive it prudent and advisable to have a Strict and Strong Watch well-Armed and under proper Discipline, and the Corporation declining to undertake the same, which we had recommended to them as the Committee appointed to wait on the Mayor Report; Therefore for the peace, good order. Safety and Protection of this City ordered that Copy's of the following Advertisement be fixed up in the proper Places in the different Wards. Notice is hereby given to the Inhabitants of the City of Albany, that it is the Opinion of their Committee that they Assemble and meet together in the different Wards of this City, at usual Places of Election to Morrow at One O Clock in the afternoon to form themselves into Companies from the Age of Sixteen to Sixty each Company to consist of a Captain Two Lieutenants, one Ensign, four Serjeants, four Corporals one Drum and fifty one Privates. By order of the Committee Dated 3rd - May I 775. Abraham Yates Chairman." "Proceedings May 3, 1775". *Minutes of the Albany Committee of Correspondence.* From Internet Archive, *Minutes of the Albany Committee of Correspondence, 1775-1778, Vol. 1.* https://archive.org/stream/MinutesOfTheAlbanyCommitteeOfCorrespondence1775-1778Vol1/MinutesOfTheAlbanyCommitteeOfCorrespondence1775-1778Vol1_djvu.txt.

brutally assaulted and imprisoned. Tories who openly criticized or challenged the rebels' motives were quickly arrested and sent off to prison.[41] Newspapers and print shops advocating loyalty to the King were immediately suppressed and shut down.

Coordinating the rebel's efforts against loyalists were a group of men known locally as the "Tory Committee". The Tory Committee's primary charge was to keep in check those loyal to the crown. Of particular interest to the committee were Scottish settlers who were not only unquestionably loyal to the English government but also routinely welcomed black slaves and local Mohawks into their parishes and churches.[42] This alarmed many local residents, especially those who either owned slaves themselves or lived within striking range of the Mohawk and Oneida tribes. To them, the recruitment of these two classes would most likely lead to either a slave revolt or Indian uprising.

---

[41] Lincoln Macveagh, *Journal of Nicholas Cresswell, 1774-1777*, (New York: The Dial Press, 1924), 147.

[42] One such minister was the Reverend Harry Munro. According to his claim, he was often subject to "frequent insults as his sentiments in favour of Great Britain were notorious." PRO AO, r. B-1160.

Economic competition also motivated the actions of the Tory Committee against Scottish settlers. As the French and Indian War drew to a close, Scottish merchants who followed and supplied the Highland regiments established their own businesses throughout Albany County. With a readily accessible customer base and network, many Scottish businessmen easily outpaced their "patriot" counterparts. With the rise in political tensions on the eve of the American Revolution, the Tory Committee seized upon an opportunity to crush their economic competitors. Merchants such as James and Alexander Robertson were all but helpless as mobs incited by the Tory Committee first shut down their print shop, then their newspaper, the *Albany Gazette*.[43] Many other merchants were physically jailed merely for suspicion of being a Tory.[44]

Following the outbreak of hostilities in 1775, many members of the New York patriot faction believed those loyal to the Crown were internal foes who needed to be carefully contained. By March of 1776, New York's Committee of Safety perceived loyalist opposition to be so

---

[43] Fraser, *Skulking*, 21-30.
[44] Ibid.

strong in certain counties, that it "advised that, in addition to disarming them [the Loyalists], their children should be taken as hostages."[45]

By the Fall of 1776, conditions in Albany County had deteriorated to the point that many loyalists started to flee northward to Canada so as to avoid continued persecution. Of course, those who remained behind were subjected to increased scrutiny and repeated interrogation before committees charged with identifying and incarcerating those loyal to the King.[46] As William Bolts accurately predicted, "history abounds with instances of nations driven into madness by the cruelty of oppression; it is the singular situation of us at present that we have been made mad by an impatience of all legal restraint and wanton abuse of power."[47]

For those loyal to the King, all efforts to remain neutral had failed and it was time to prepare for war.

---

[45] *New York Historical Society Collections, Lee Papers* Volume 5, (New York: Printed for the Society, 1868-1924), vol. 1, 213-215.

[46] For example, see the Minutes of the Schenectady Committee 1775-1779. On May 10, 1777, under intense questioning, a suspected Tory denied being a Tory so as to avoid incarceration. Unfortunately, his fate was sealed when refused to renounce his allegiance to the King ("As one [man] protested he was no Tory, but was a man for the King").

[47] William Bolts, *Consideration on Indian Affairs*, (London: Brotherton and Sewell in Cornhill, 1772), viii.

Chapter Four: The Hampshire Land Grants

Complicating tensions between loyalist and patriot factions in New York and New England was an ongoing dispute over land grants located in modern day western Vermont. From 1690 until 1815, this corridor of land was known as the "Hampshire Grants" and was the scene of continuous warfare and civil unrest. Following France's defeat in the French and Indian War, the Hampshire Grants was flooded with New Englanders, Scottish and Irish immigrants, New Yorkers and veteran soldiers all seeking new economic opportunities. Prominent loyalists, including Daniel McAlpin and Ebenezer Jessup, acquired large tracts of land within the territory. However, when settlers arrived with land titles in hand, many found conflicting claims to the same land held by other settlers. Violence quickly followed.

The source of the land disputes could be traced back to the aftermath of King George's War. In 1749, Governor Benning Wentworth of the Colony of New Hampshire asserted that New Hampshire's south western boundary line met at the juncture of the Hudson and Mohawk Rivers. In turn, the governor initiated the sale of land grants in territories west of the Connecticut River. Many of these grants were sold to land speculators at £20 per grant. Unfortunately for Wentworth, the Colony of New York also laid claim to the same region. New York asserted its southern border with Connecticut existed twenty miles east of the Hudson, while its border with New Hampshire was placed at the Connecticut River. As with New Hampshire, the Colony of New York also initiated the sale of land patents to speculators and wealthy colonists.

Settlers quickly arrived in the disputed territories. New York colonists were alarmed when they discovered New Hampshire settlers creating townships further and further westward, while New Hampshire colonists objected to encroachments by New Yorkers. By September 1762, tensions between the two colonies rose when New York settlers apprehended New Hampshire surveyors examining potential land grants on the eastern shore of Lake Champlain. In response, Governor Wentworth issued a proclamation re-establishing his colony's claim to the Hampshire Grants.[48] New York immediately appealed to the Board of Trade, requesting a confirmation of their original land grant. In 1764, the Board of Trade resolved the dispute in favor of New York. That same year a royal order issued confirmed the Board of Trade's ruling and declared that the Hampshire Grants were part of New York. By March, 1772, the Hampshire Grants were formally incorporated into New York's Charlotte County.[49]

Upon receipt of the order, New Hampshire ceased issuing land grants. However, this did little to alleviate tensions on the local level. New Hampshire settlers refused to recognize the authority of New York colony while New York settlers quickly moved to eject the "illegal"

---

[48] In support of his position, Wentworth relied upon the New Hampshire Letters Patent of 1741.

[49] Charlotte County was created on March 12, 1772 from Northern Albany County. The county included all of Lakes George and Champlain, the eastern Adirondack Mountains, the headwaters of the Hudson River, and present day western Vermont. The county seat was Fort Edward.

occupiers of their land holdings. British Captain John Montresor observed with some frustration "some scores of Families have arrived and settled there living on Hunting and Fishing chiefly and now beginning to cultivate their land. They declare that possession is Eleven points in the Law and that they will take the advantage of these Disturbances and as no law prevails at present."[50]

1777 Map of Charlotte County and Incorporated Hampshire Grants

[50] John Montresor, and James Gabriel Montresor, *The Montresor Journals, Volume 14* ed. G.D. Skull (New York: Printed for the New York Historical Society, 1881), 367.

In 1771, the New York Royal Governor William Tryon and private land speculators offered thousands of acres worth of new land grants for sale within the vicinity of Crown Point and Lake Champlain. The population of the Hampshire Grants exploded as more English and Irish veterans of the French and Indian War, as well as Scottish immigrants and Connecticut and New Jersey colonists, flooded into the territory. Of course, the growing population only served to rekindle land disputes and sparked further confrontations. On June 11, 1771, over a dozen armed men, led by Robert Cochran and supported by New Hampshire grantees, forcibly removed a New York settler from his three hundred fifty acre tract of land, attacked several of his neighbors and burned their homes. In response, Governor Tryon warned authorities that unless the problem of conflicting land titles was resolved, "the daring insults of these people will in a short time lead to serious consequences."[51]

Almost two years later, on April 21, 1773, British soldiers stationed at Crown Point and under the command of a Captain Anstruther

---

[51] Eugene R. Fingerhut, *The Other New York, the American Revolution Beyond New York City, 1763-1787*, (Albany: State University of New York Press, 2005), 185.

accidentally set fire to a barracks chimney while making soap. The fire quickly spread and ignited the garrison's magazine. Following the explosion, local New Englanders descended upon the fort and plundered it. Shortly thereafter, "New Hampshire Rioters" led by Ethan Allen embarked on a campaign of terror to drive out settlers with ties to New York. The stability of the region deteriorated to the point that many New York settlers abandoned plans to reside on designated land grants, New Englanders built block houses on the eastern shore of Lake Champlain, and British authorities deliberated as to whether or not a military expedition should be dispatched into the Hampshire Grants to quell the violence.[52]

Unfortunately, before stability could be restored to the region, the Revolutionary War started and the Hampshire Grants was thrown into even greater turmoil. Unlike loyalists and patriots in other parts of New

---

[52] Ibid, 182-183. In desperation, the New York Council sought from Gen. Thomas Gage, the army commander-in-chief for North America and governor of Massachusetts, two hundred troops to re-establish control over the region the "New Hampshire Rioters" were terrorizing. Gage instead wrote the England for instructions, and in November 1774 he received orders to merely repair the forts at Crown Point and Ticonderoga.

York and New England, allegiances to the crown or congress in the Hampshire Grants was often dictated by land claims and economic opportunity rather than social, cultural or religious principles. According to Paul R. Huey, contributing author of *The Other New York: The American Revolution Beyond New York City 1763-1787*, at the outset of the war, many inhabitants of the Hampshire Grants were more concerned with their respective land grants than the revolutionary crisis.[53] In turn, these property interests guided whether or not one would maintain loyalty to the British government or support the revolutionary movement. Communities became sharply divided, competing militia and paramilitary organizations were raised and bloody skirmishes flared up. By 1777, much of the Hampshire Grants near Fort Edward and along the shores of Lake Champlain were "marked with Devastation, and of the many pleasant habitations ... some were burnt, others torn to Pieces and rendered unfit for Use, and but a few of the meanest occupied: the Inhabitants in general having been forced to leave their once peaceful Dwellings to

---

[53] Fingerhut, *The Other New York*, 198.

escape the Rage of War. Thus this once agreeable and delightful Part of the Country now displayed a most shocking Picture of Havock and wild Desolation."[54]

---

[54] Richard Cartwright Jr. *A Journey to Canada, c. 1777*. Journal. From
http://www.62ndregiment.org/A_Journey_to_Canada_by_Cartwright.pdf

Chapter Five: The Flight North

Following the outbreak of the American Revolution in 1775, General William Howe quickly moved to organize an appropriate response to the deteriorating situation in New York and New England. One early initiative he undertook to was to encourage retired military officers Captain Alexander McDonald and Major William Edmeston to recruit veterans who would assist with operations against the American rebellion.[55] According to period documents, Howe authorized Major Edmeston to raise a battalion of soldiers from the Albany, Charlotte and Tryon County regions with "instructions to engage the Men taking care not to appoint more than one Captain, two Subalterns, three sergeants, three Corporals and one Drummer for every fifty men." McDonald assisted the major in his recruiting efforts.

---

[55] (SOURCE?)

Unfortunately, the work of both men was quickly discovered by rebel authorities. McDonald was forced to flee north to Canada while Edmeston was arrested and sent to Massachusetts.[56] The responsibility of continuing to raise a loyalist corps for General Howe fell upon one Captain Daniel McAlpin.[57]

---

[56] Major Edmeston was a resident of German Flatts, New York. On May 28, 1777, the Tyron Committee resolved that this "half pay officer of the King of G. Britain" be arrested and taken to Albany where General Schuyler could determine his disposition. Schuyler kept Edmeston in Albany until mid-October and then ordered him sent to Berkshire County, Massachusetts with a number of other Tory prisoners. By the end of 1777, Major Edmeston had returned to England.

[57] "To His Excellency Frederick Haldimand, Esq. Governor General of Canada and Territories thereon depending General and Commander in Chief of all His Majesty's Forces therein, etc. The Memorial of Captain Daniel McAlpin of the 60th Regiment humbly sheweth Your Excellency's Memorialist having in concert with Lieutenant Colonel William Edmonston of the 48th Regiment proposed a plan for raising a battalion of his Majesty's loyal subjects in Albany and in the neighboring counties. Such plan was laid before General Sir William Howe and His Excellency was pleased to approve of the same and he gave this instructions to engage the men, taking care not to appoint more than one captain, two subalterns, three sergeants, three corporals, and one drummer to every 50 men. In consequence of General Howe's instructions your Excellency's Memorialist employed proper people at a considerable expense to engage volunteers for this service and he was so successful that in six months' time five hundred and seventy-two men were engaged, two hundred of which number joined General Burgoyne's army as will appear by a certificate signed by the Deputy Commissary of Musters. Your Excellency's Memorialist did appoint Mr. Peter Drumond to be captain of a company and several other good men to be subalterns. Captain Drummond had the misfortune to be taken prisoner in the field of battle on the 19th September 1777 when he was exerting himself in the execution of his duty and he has since suffered much, being a long time confined in irons in a dungeon. As your Excellency" Memorialist did not appoint but one captain, five lieutenants, five ensigns, and one quarter master to the above number of men he humbly hopes that your Excellency will be good enough to support them in those

After forty years of service in the British Army, including a stint in the 60th Regiment of Foot, Captain Daniel McAlpin retired from military life and settled in Stillwater, New York, with his wife Mary and three children James, Isabella and Mary. In May of 1774 he purchased approximately one thousand acres of land located on the west side of Saratoga Lake near the present town of Malta, New York. His first house was built on site in 1775, while a second was constructed in 1776.[58]

Following the Battles of Lexington and Concord, local authorities actively courted McAlpin to serve as an officer with the Continental Army. To the rebels, McAlpin was a respected authority who had the potential to recruit countless men on behalf of the American cause for independence. However, McAlpin rejected their overtures. It is possible he declined the offer because of the Scottish cultural norm of unwavering loyalty to the crown. It is more likely his motivations were financial.

---

different stations as they have sacrificed all they had for their loyalty. Quebec, 18 November, 1778 (Signed) Daniel McAlpin, Captain 60th Regiment." Memorial of Daniel McAlpin, November 18, 1778, Public Archives of Canada, B Series, Volume 214, 84.

[58] Both houses were timber log planked and floored. The houses were valued at £100 and £200 respectively. A value of £1 Sterling per acre unimproved and £2.10 Sterling improved was placed on the land. By the summer of 1777 there were at least 170 acres in high cultivation. Captain McAlpin had 20-25 servants in constant employ on his farm.

Specifically, McAlpin was embroiled in a bitter dispute over a six thousand acre tract of land that he had acquired along the Connecticut River in the Hampshire Grants. As was the case with many other New York landholders, settlers from New England seized his property and claimed it as their own. McAlpin appealed to the Colony of New York, requested crown authorities to intervene on his behalf and declare him the rightful owner. As a result, Captain McAlpin needed the King's continued jurisdiction over the Hampshire Grants if he was ever to take repossession of his disputed property again.[59]

Unfortunately, by 1775, a decision on his claim was still pending. Recognizing the inherent risk of losing his six thousand acres if he sided with rebels, McAlpin attempted to delay giving a decision for almost a year. However, by June 1776, McAlpin was called out by local rebel leaders and was forced to reject their invitation to join the American

---

[59] Fraser, *Skulking*, 31-32.

Both houses were timber log planked and floored. The houses were valued at £100 and £200 respectively. A value of £1 Sterling per acre unimproved and £2.10 Sterling improved was placed on the land. By the summer of 1777 there were at least 170 acres in high cultivation. Captain McAlpin had 20-25 servants in constant employ on his farm. Ibid.

cause. McAlpin was promptly arrested and sent to a jail in Albany.

On July 26, 1776, Albany's Tory Committee declared that McAlpin was to be sent to Redhook, New York in preparation for transfer to a prison mine in Connecticut.[60] However, the order was revoked due to McAlpin's quickly deteriorating health. In August, 1776, American General Philip Schuyler personally intervened on behalf of McAlpin and ordered him released. In support of this order, Schuyler declared "little or no harm might be expected from him."[61]

Jessup's Men

Daniel McAlpin returned to his homestead and by September 1776 he was recruiting men for the British Army stationed in Canada. Less than

---

[60] "Proceedings July 26, 1776". *Minutes of the Albany Committee of Correspondence.* From Internet Archive, *Minutes of the Albany Committee of Correspondence, 1775-1778, Vol. 1.* https://archive.org/stream/MinutesOfTheAlbanyCommitteeOfCorrespondence1775-1778Vol1/MinutesOfTheAlbanyCommitteeOfCorrespondence1775-1778Vol1_djvu.txt. It was most likely the prison was the notorious Simsbury Mines of Simsbury, Connecticut.

[61] "Proceedings, August 24, 1776." From Internet Archive, *Minutes of the Albany Committee of Correspondence, 1775-1778, Vol. 1.* https://archive.org/stream/MinutesOfTheAlbanyCommitteeOfCorrespondence1775-1778Vol1/MinutesOfTheAlbanyCommitteeOfCorrespondence1775-1778Vol1_djvu.txt.

a month later, McAlpin had successfully enlisted fifty-six men who were quietly dispatched northward without him.[62] At some point in their journey towards Canada, they encountered Daniel McAlpin's primary competitors for the recruitment of local men to fight for the crown: the Jessup brothers.

Edward and Ebenezer Jessup were born in Stamford, Connecticut. In 1743 the family relocated with their father to Dutchess County, New York. On the eve of the American Revolution, the Jessup Brothers were counted among the wealthiest men in the Hudson River Valley. The brothers owned a ferry service, several saw and grist mills and a large tract of land situated where the Schroon and Sacandaga Rivers joined the Hudson in Charlotte County.[63] Politicians and government officials, including New York's Governor William Tyron, courted the men while land speculators actively sought their services and expertise.

---

[62] Peter Drummond, *Drummond to Haldimand, November 13, 1780*. Letter. From Haldimand Papers, AddMss 21827, Part 1, f. 218. See Appendix A for a roster of those men who were with Jessup in 1776.

[63] Known as Jessup's Landing, the homesteads were located in present day Corinth, New York.

Horrified by both the passage of the Declaration of Independence and witnessing multiple loyalists being subjected to considerable abuse at the hands of "patriot" neighbors, Ebenezer Jessup quickly obtained Governor Tyron's assent to raise men in support of His Majesty's government. With the help of his brother, Edward Jessup, the men recruited twenty-four men and prepared to join the British army. Of course, when the two encountered the fifty-six men raised by McAlpin, they recognized an opportunity and claimed the men as their own.[64]

Shortly afterwards, the Jessup brothers and their recruits started a thirty-six mile journey towards General Carleton's army stationed at Crown Point. When the brothers arrived, they boarded the warship *HMS Maria,* and informed Carleton that their band of men wished to join his army and "conquer our enemies and reestablish civil government for the

---

[64] Whether McAlpin's recruits willingly joined the Jessups or were ultimately placed under the Jessups' command by Carleton upon arrival at Crown Point is unknown. Gavin Watt, a prominent loyalist historian, subscribes to the theory that Carleton placed the men recruited by McAlpin under the command of Jessup upon their arrival at Crown Point. In support of his theory, Mr. Watt asserts, quite logically, that McAlpin and the Jessups were competitors for the recruitment of men and McAlpin never would have allowed men raised by him to be turned over to the Jessups.

honour of the Crown and the true interest of the Colonies."[65] Carleton was less than receptive to the proposal and worse, unimpressed. From his perspective, the Tory refugees posed a drain on critical supplies and finances slated for his troops. More importantly, he believed these men should have remained at home waiting for the arrival of a British army of liberation.[66]

Nevertheless, these eighty odd men were now at Crown Point and Carleton had to deal with them. With some reservations, he accepted the refugees into the British Army, placed them on the appropriate pay rolls[67]

---

[65] Ebenezer Jessup, *Memorial of Ebenezer Jessup, February 1, 1778.* From Great Britain, British Library, Additional Manuscripts, No. 21827, folio 145-146. http://www.royalprovincial.com/military/rhist/kla/klamem1.htm

[66] "Sir Guy Carleton to Maj. Gen. Phillips. Head Quarters at Quebec . . . Sir: The plan approved by Gov. Tyron as Mr. Jessop reports seems to me very judicious; it is to be wished this Gentleman and his followers had remained at their own homes till it remained practicable; it cannot now take place before next summer; in the meantime I should recommend it to them to join Sir John Johnson's regiment and enclosed is an order for Major Grey to take them under his command." Lieutenant James N., Royal Artillery Hadden, *Journal and Orderly Books*, (Albany: 1884), 69.

[67] "Sir Guy Carleton to Mr. Jessup. Head Quarters at Quebec . . . Sir: I am commanded to acquaint you that Sir Guy Carleton has received your letter of the 5th Instant and will in a few days answer it fully; in the meantime His Excellency desires you will send him a list of the persons who accompany you, and the particulars of the information which you mention to have given relative to the operations of General Howe's army &c.. General Phillips not having transmitted them." Ibid. Each refugee was entitled to 6d per day, Halifax currency, less rations, clothing and hospital expenses. "Halifax currency" was

and ordered them to join the King's Royal Regiment in Point Claire, Canada.[68] However, acceptance into the army came with conditions. Carleton warned the Jessups that their recruits would be treated as "refugees than as soldiers" and any arrangements made were "merely an asylum" so the refugees could draw rations, clothing and other supplies necessary for survival.[69] Jessup and his recruits were then sent one hundred and twenty miles north to Chateauguay, Quebec to be billeted.

Surprisingly, the Jessup and their men objected to the placement.[70] According to Carleton, "I informed your Lordship that this Army had been joined at Crown Point by parties of the loyal inhabitants of the adjacent Provinces, who had fled from the persecution they were suffering in the

---

worth less than the sterling used to pay regular troops. It was also ordered that "boys of 15 or younger and old men" also be clothed, fed and housed. Theodore Corbett, *No Turning Point: The Saratoga Campaign in Perspective*, (Oklahoma: University of Oklahoma Press, 2012), 91. See note 39 which references, among other primary sources, Gray to Jessup, August 10, 1785.

[68] By January 12, 1777, many of the recruits had not arrived at Pointe Claire and lingered behind at Chateauguay because of smallpox. James Gray, *Gray to Carleton, Jan. 12, 1777*. Letter. From Haldimand Papers, B-158, 9. On December 1, 1776, Carleton ordered Adjutant General Foy that the Jessup party "be provided for by General Phillips".

[69] Hadden, *Journal and Orderly Books*, 69.

[70] From the perspective of the Jessup brothers, the recruits they brought with them formed the nucleus of a new provincial regiment.

places of their residence; during the winter their numbers have increased considerably; a body of near a hundred came here under the conduct of a Mr. Jessup of the province of New York, his brother and several other men of some note in the neighbourhood of Albany. They have all been sent to Sir John Johnson's Corps, but being of a different part of the country, they desired not to be drafted into that Regiment."[71] Instead, Jessup's men demanded that they be treated as their own corps and in the tradition of the local militia, serve under officers of their own choosing. Carleton immediately rejected the demand and on January 14, 1777, ordered Major James Gray of the King's Royal Regiment to administer oaths of allegiance to the refugees and arrest those who refused.[72] All of the men subsequently signed the oath.

However, by the end of January, the men were still objecting to any placement with Sir Johnson's Corps and began to refer to themselves as "Jessup's Corps". Following several letters of complaint from Major

---

[71] Sir Guy Carleton, *Carleton to Germain, May 27, 1777*. Letter. From Ernest A. Cruikshank , and Gavin K. Watt, *The King's Royal Regiment of New York* , (Toronto: 1984), 15.
[72] Sir Guy Carleton, *Carleton to Gray, January 14, 1777*. Letter

Gray, Carleton quickly discovered that the "corps" had, without authorization, organized itself into three companies commanded by Edward Jessup, Jonathan Jones and Ebenezer Jessup.[73] Exasperated, Carleton complained "I know of no such thing as Jessup's Corps, mentioned by Major Gray". Worse yet, the General was horrified to discover the Jessup brothers were travelling throughout the Canadian countryside attempting to recruit men from other provincial units.[74]

Ultimately, Carleton relented and permitted the Jessup's to form their own provincial regiment, entitled Ebenezer Jessup's Corps of King's Loyal Americans. Not surprisingly, Jessup's Corps continued to be a constant source of frustration for the British command. In March, 1777, a Major Gray complained "those men join'd Jessups Core gives me more truble then I ever had."[75] The next month, the same major bitterly asserted "I have been thirty Years a soldier, but never had so much trouble as with

---

[73] General Sir Frederick Haldimand, *Muster Roll of the King's Loyal Americans from the Province of New York, at Point Clair, January 24, 1777*. From Haldimand Papers, B-167, 5. By August, 1777 Jessup's Corps was comprised of at least four companies.

[74] Hadden, *Journal and Orderly Books*, 71.

[75] James Gray, *Gray to Foy, March 24, 1777*. Letter. From Haldimand Papers, B-158, 642.

those fellows; I have try'd every Method to please them, & to show them the Generals good intentions towards them."[76]

From its inception, Jessup's Corps was in desperate need of clothing and equipment. As a result, General Carleton ordered Major Gray to acquire clothing for Jessup's men and encouraged the major to locate "some cheap uniform clothing to keep them from the severity of the weather".[77] In turn, the major travelled to Montreal and had purchased "on behalf of Messr Jessup and his followers" regimental coats. As Gray would later note, the coats were "the cheapest that could be got, at Montreal, very Common red stuff turn'd up with Green as Red seemed to be their favorite colour, and being got rather than any other I gratified their taste."[78] If Major Gray's comments are interpreted correctly, the coats

---

[76] Ibid, 643. It is possible that these complaints would contribute to Daniel McAlpin's political advantage over the Jessup brothers in the years to come.

[77] "Major Gray... may either cloath them [Jessup's people] as the Royal Reg't of New York, or buy them
some cheap uniform cloathing to keep them from the severity of the weather as you shall be pleased to direct." Hadden, *Journal and Orderly Books*, 69.

[78] James Gray, *Gray to Haldimand, January 11, 1777*. Letter.

purchased were sufficient to cloth all of the recruits then present in Canada

under Jessup, including the men drafted by McAlpin.[79]

In April 1777, as additional recruits poured into Canada, Gray

made a second attempt to procure coats for men drawn into Jessup's

Corps. As with the January purchase, he was forced to buy the same

cheap coats from the same supplier. Nevertheless, the major was able to

successfully clothe all but eight of Jessup's recruits.[80] Inexplicably, Gray

complained to his superiors that unless ordered, he would not purchase

---

[79] The full text of Gray's report to Carleton states "Some time ago I received your Excellency's orders and directions concerning the Messrs Jessups and followers, according to those, & Major General Phillips's I have acted; *Bought them an uniform* the cheapest that could be got at Montreal, very common Red Stuff turn'd up with Green; as Red seemed to be their favourite colour and being got rather cheaper than any other I gratified their taste." Gray does not qualify his statement that he purchased coats for some or part of Jessup's men. Instead, he asserts he "bought them" coats. If one looks at this statement in conjunction with Carleton's November 29, 1776 order, one could correctly assert that Gray clothed all of Jessup's recruits present in Canada in 1776.
[80] "You'll find by the Merchants accounts sent you for Cloathing, that the Messrs Jessups' party & the Twenty Seven Men that Petition'd the General were all provided for, but there was Adam's & his Eight Men who are still unprovided for, as they at that time wou'd not accept of the Cloathing, tho' Adams has now agreed to join as a Lieut in Jessups Corp, Yet there's Eight Suits of Cloaths wanted to compleat the Royalists under my Command, they are now willing to take the Cloathing, which I have not to give till I am ordered to buy for them." James Gray, *James Gray to ?, April 20, 1777.* Letter.

additional coats for the corps.[81]

Clothing was not the only issue Jessup's Corps faced. Many of the recruits who arrived in Canada were unarmed and poorly equipped. As a result, the British government was forced to secure weapons and accoutrements for Jessup's men. It is likely Carleton ordered outdated Model 1728 French infantry muskets left over from the previous French and Indian War and sitting in storage in Quebec be issued to Jessup's men rather than newer Second Model infantry muskets.[82] Period accounts also

---

[81] Ibid.

[82] "Sorel 26th July 1779. Sir, I am favoured with your letter of the 20th Instant. I am happy If I was able to do my duty to merit His Excellencys Approbation. When I got the Command of the Corps of Loyalists the most of them were then & are still Employed in the works, Sundays not Excepted, and I had no oppertunity to see them under arms, Except Capt. Leakes Detachment whose arms I found in very bad order, Sir John Jonson and Capt. Leake undertook to report this to His Excellency The Commander in Chief. Upon Examining the arms of the remainder of the Corps left here I found them much in the same Condition. I have lately received a Letter from Captain Leake wherein he wishes much to have the arms of his Detachment Exchanged he reports them all unfit for Service. The most part of all those arms were not good when we received them, being old french muskets without Baynets no Dout they were neglected by those people who assume the rank of officers which makes them still worse. At the same time If it be convenient to His Excellency to order Compleat good arms to be Delivered to the whole of our Effectives. I Shall while I have the honor to Command them, use my best endeavours to have the arms always keept in good and Serviceable order. I need not Explain to His Excellency the figure an old Greyheaded fellow will make at the head of a parcel undisciplined people with bad arms in their hands'. My old withered face Blushes at the thought of it. I hope the General will be Good Enough to prevent me appearing in

suggest that many of Jessup's men received partial "stands of arms" in the form of belly boxes and belting.

Colonel Edward Jessup's Cartridge Box

this mortifying Situation by ordering good arms to be Delivered to us. I Shall Esteem it a particular favour if His Excellency will be good Enough to grant me leave to be the bearer of my next monthly return myself. I have business at Quebec that requires my going there soon. I am with great regard and Esteem Sir Your most obedient Humble Servant Danl. McAlpin Capt. 60th Regt., Commanding the Loyalists Robert Mathews Esqr. Secty. to His Excellency the Commander in Chief at Quebec" Daniel McAlpin, *McAlpin to Haldimand, July 26, 1779.* Letter. From Great Britain, British Library, Additional Manuscripts, No. 21821, folios 29-30.

According to research conducted by Jim Kochan, Burgoyne and Carleton nearly exhausted the supply of firelocks stored at Quebec in the summer, 1776 by arming provincials under the command of Johnson, Canadian militia and recruits from the Royal Highland Emigrants. Although it appears the supply was replenished at some point in 1777, Burgoyne nearly depleted it again in September, 1777 when he received almost one thousand stands of British and French arms slated for unarmed provincials under his command.

Bayonets were in short supply and as Daniel McAlpin would later assert, many of the loyalists who served during the Burgoyne Campaign were equipped with "Old French muskets without baynets."[83] It is unknown what additional equipment Jessup's men received if any. Nevertheless, by May, 1777, General Carleton was satisfied that the corps was sufficiently equipped and supplied for the coming military expedition.[84]

Daniel McAlpin's Recruits

While McAlpin's first set of recruits were in Canada under the command of Colonel Ebenezer Jessup, Captain McAlpin was still at work in Albany County drafting additional men for the King. Despite being forced to flee from his home by rebel mobs and hide in nearby woods for over two weeks in February, 1777, the Tory leader was still able to successfully recruit over 570 men. Unfortunately, local rebels quickly

[83] Ibid.

[84] On May 27, 1777, Sir Guy Carleton wrote to Germain to confirm the men of Peter and Jessup's Corps were clothed and armed by the British Army under the guidance of Major Gray. He further detailed that pay scales for the Corps were established for enlisted men, non-commissioned officers and officers.

learned of the plot. A bounty of $100 was set for the capture of McAlpin and four of his ringleaders.[85] Captain Tyrannis Collins of the Albany County Militia was ordered to arrest McAlpin and "carry [those] who were supposed to be disaffected to the country, as prisoners to Albany."[86]

Realizing he had been exposed, McAlpin was forced to flee to the safety of Canada with less than thirty of his recruits. The band of men retreated west towards the Adirondack Mountains and the safety of the Jessup's lands; hot in pursuit were a combined force of Albany County militia and a regiment of Green Mountain Boys.[87]

It appears this group of loyalists were armed and equipped, for a skirmish erupted when the pursuers finally caught up with McAlpin. "There was a battle fought by . . . some loyalists against rebels from Schenectady and some Yankees in which we lost one man, five wounded

---

[85] "Proceedings April 17, 1777". *Minutes of the Albany Committee of Correspondence.* From Internet Archive, *Minutes of the Albany Committee of Correspondence, 1775-1778, Vol. 1.* From *https*://archive.org/stream/MinutesOfTheAlbanyCommitteeOfCorrespondence1775-1778Vol1/MinutesOfTheAlbanyCommitteeOfCorrespondence1775-1778Vol1_djvu.txt.
[86] Fraser, *Skulking,* 35.
[87] Ibid.

and eleven taken prisoners which were confin'd in Albany."[88] In the

confusion, McAlpin and twelve of his followers managed to escape. They

hid in the woods somewhere between Jessup's Patent and Crown Point for

a week before locating a suitable cave to take refuge in.[89] Afterwards,

McAlpin made an attempt to free the eleven prisoners, but was

unsuccessful.[90] The loyalists remained in hiding until Burgoyne's army

arrived at Fort Edward in August, 1777.

William Fraser's Recruits

When Captain McAlpin was forced to flee, he turned to William

Fraser to continue the recruitment of loyalists. A prosperous farmer from

Ball's Town, Fraser secretly recruited forty men on behalf of McAlpin.

However, a rebel spy learned of the recruitment scheme and reported it to

---

[88] Haldimand Papers, Additional Manuscripts No. 21875, folio 218.

[89] AO, Volume 131, reel number B-2189; "Proceedings April 17, 1777". *Minutes of the Albany Committee of Correspondence.* From Internet Archive, *Minutes of the Albany Committee of Correspondence, 1775-1778, Vol. 1.*
https://archive.org/stream/MinutesOfTheAlbanyCommitteeOfCorrespondence1775-1778Vol1/MinutesOfTheAlbanyCommitteeOfCorrespondence1775-1778Vol1_djvu.txt.

[90] "We sent a petition for the release of the prisoners with threatening to fetch them. The Committee refused us and kept the men we sent with the . . . prisoners." Haldimand Papers, Additional Manuscripts No. 21875, folio 218.

Colonel James Gordon, commander of an Ulster County militia regiment. Gordon, in turn, mobilized his regiment to arrest Fraser and his recruits.

Fraser immediately recognized the danger he and his men were in. The men fled to a patch of woods north of Ball's Town where they waited almost ten days for a guide from the British Army to lead them to General Burgoyne. When the group realized the scout would not be coming, they began to trek north, following "infrequented and impassable ways."[91] Twenty miles into their journey, a party of American militia ambushed them. Hoping to escape the trap, Fraser led his men to Jessup's Little Falls.

According to period accounts, the upper Hudson River was forced into a narrow corridor of black limestone and led to Jessup's Little Falls - a waterfall with a sixty foot drop. Across the chute was a thirteen foot single plank which served as a footbridge.[92] Regrettably, Fraser's attempt to cross the falls failed and all but one man was captured. Their arms and

---

[91] AO, Volume 29, reel number B-1162.
[92] Fraser, *Skulking*, 39.

equipment were seized and later sold for profit in Albany.[93] The group

was marched back to Albany and promptly thrown into a jail below town

hall. According to Fraser, "They were not treated as prisoners of war, but

handcuffed like ordinary criminals . . . the rebels did not undertake to feed

their prisoners and it was custom for [Tory families] to come every day to

the gaol with provisions."[94] One by one, Fraser's recruits were brought

before the Tory Committee, tried and found guilty. All but William Fraser

were ordered to remain jailed until payment of a fifteen dollar fine was

received and an oath to the State of New York was given. Fraser was

---

[93] Memorial of Alexander Laughlen, July 12, 1789. Public Archives of Canada.
http://familytreemaker.genealogy.com/users/b/r/u/Judith-D-Bruder-MO/WEBSITE-
0001/UHP-1090.html. "The Memorial of Alexander Laughlen humbly sheweth that
whereas in the year one thousand seven hundred and seventy-four he left Stirlingshire in
Scotland and came to America, that he settled in Ballstown, State of New York and that
in the year one thousand seven hundred and seventy-seven having voluntarily joined a
party of loyalists, was enlisted under Captain McAlpin and was put under the direction of
Captain William Fraser and Lieutenant Thomas Fraser who had the command of said
party on their way to Canada. That after ten days' march the party was surprised by the
Rebells, taken prisoners and conducted to Albany."; Statement of William and Thomas
Fraser in Support of Alexander Laughlen's Land Petition, February 9, 1798. "I hereby
Certify that the bearer Alex Laughlen has been taken prisoner with us when endeavored
to come to canada in the spring 1777 and carried prisoner to Albany and from thence to
New England where he suffered mutch for his loyalty and attachment to the British
government."
[94] AO, Volume 29, reel number B-1162.

sentenced to one year in jail.[95]

Shortly after these hearings, Fraser's wife arrived at the jail with her husband's daily provisions. Inside a loaf of bread was a file and coil of rope. After some effort, Fraser and twenty of his men were able to break free of their shackles, remove at least one of the iron bars on the jail's window and escape.[96] Unarmed and without provisions, the men fled from Albany towards Fort Edward. Like McAlpin and his men, Fraser's company was forced to remain in hiding until the arrival of General Burgoyne.

---

[95] Ibid.

[96] Ibid. Not all of Fraser's men were successful in the prison break. "This is to Certify all Gentlemen Whom It may Concern That Alexander Laughlen Was a good faithful Subject To King George during the Last Rebellion and Sufered Domstick Vilence by the hands of the Userpeis Was taking Prisoner Going to the British And Was keep three years In Close Confinement Which was a Very hard fate And Now means to maake his Residence under protection of King George." Statement of James Dearin in Support of Alexander Laughlen's Land Petition. February, 1798. After the escape, those prisoners who were left behind were transferred to jails in New York, Connecticut, Massachusetts, New Hampshire and Pennsylvania.

Chapter Six: The Plight of the Female Loyalist

Historian Janice Potter McKinnon, in her authoritative work *While the Women Only Wept*, observed that in the 18th Century, most American and English women were bound by the legal and moral codes of their respective communities. Life was not easy for women. From the perspective of society, women were assumed to be helpless because they were like children who could not provide the basic necessities for themselves, but had to rely on men for food, shelter, and clothing. It was assumed women could not take care of themselves and thus, were treated as helpless inferiors who were expected to view themselves in such terms.[97]

Women were often dependent upon the companionship of their sisters and other female relatives. Siblings often spent countless hours

---

[97] Janice Potter McKinnon, *While the Women Only Wept*, (Montreal: 1993), 8.

spinning, preparing food, making soap and working in the field. They also

assisted each other in the birthing and raising of children.[98]

Often the major decision in a woman's life was the choice of a

mate. Although 18th century women had some say in the selection of a

spouse, parents still played a significant role in the decision and their

consent was required.[99] Colonial era women were expected to obey their

husbands, rear the children, cook and prepare meals, make and launder

clothes and undertake minor household repairs.[100] They were often

pregnant on their wedding days and received little protection from

domestic violence.[101] In short, a married woman was seen as subordinate

to her husband.

---

[98] McKinnon, *While the Women*, 6.

[99] Ibid, 5.

[100] By comparison, a female camp follower in an 18th Century British regiment was considered an integral part of the organization. Most were gainfully employed as sutlers, nurses and laundresses, received financial compensation for their contributions and often had their own lodgings.

[101] "The husband also (by the old law) might give his wife moderate correction. For, as he is to answer for her misbehaviour, the law thought it reasonable to intrust him with this power of restraining her, by domestic chastisement, in the same moderation that a man is allowed to correct his servants or children; for whom the master or parent is also liable in some cases to answer. But this power of correction was confined within reasonable bounds; and the husband was prohibited to use any violence to his wife, "[here translated:] other than as licitly and reasonably pertains to the husband for the rule and

Central to the marriage contract was the dual notion that the man had the sole power to make important decisions for the family unit and the responsibility to ensure its well-being by providing the essentials - food, clothing, and housing.[102] Under the eyes of the colonial and English law, a married woman often could not vote, collect wages, make contracts, testify in court, serve as a juror, buy or sell property nor execute a will on her own. As eighteenth century legal scholar Sir William Blackstone surmised:

> By marriage, the husband and wife are one person in law: that is, the very being or legal existence of the woman is suspended during the marriage, or at least is incorporated and consolidated into that of the husband: under whose wing, protection, and *cover* she performs every thing; and is therefore called in our law-French a *feme-covert*; is said to be *covert-baron*, or under the protection and influence of her

---

correction of his wife." The civil law gave the husband the same, or a larger, authority over his wife; allowing him, for some misdemesnors, "[here translated:] with flails and cudgels to beat the wife energetically;" for others, only "[here translated:] to apply limited punishment." But, with us, in the politer reign of Charles the second, this power of correction began to be doubted: and a wife may now have security of the peace against her husband; or, in return, a husband against his wife. Yet the lower rank of people, who were always fond of the old common law, still claim and exert their ancient privilege: and the courts of law will still permit a husband to restrain a wife of her liberty, in case of any gross misbehaviour." William Blackstone, *Commentaries on the Laws of England*, (London: 1765), 442-445.

[102] Ibid, 7.

husband, her *baron*, or lord . . . [Though] our law in general considers man and wife as one person, yet there are some instances in which she is . . . considered; as inferior to him, and acting by his compulsion. And therefore all deeds executed, and acts done, by her . . . are void, or at least voidable; except it be a fine, or the like matter of record, in which case she must be solely and secretly examined, to learn if her act be voluntary. She cannot by will devise lands to her husband, unless under special circumstances; for at the time of making it she is supposed to be under his coercion. And in some felonies, and other inferior crimes, committed by her, though constraint of her husband, the law excuses her: but this extends not to treason or murder.[103]

Historical evidence suggests married colonial women, appeared to accept their subordinate position within the family. Rather than complaining or contemplating the unfairness of their situation, married women knew that their role was to accept their lot in life and do their duty. As loyalist Dothe Stone recalled "I was obliged and did affect cheerfulness in my behavior . . . I answered with a smile when my heart was ready to break. . . [I] must submit when it comes to open things."[104]

---

[103] Blackstone, *Commentaries*, 442-445.

[104] Dothe Stone, *Dothe Stone Diary, October 22, 1783*, Journal. From the Archives of Ontario, MS 519, reel 1; Ibid, October 24, 1783.
http://webcache.googleusercontent.com/search?q=cache:http://joelstone.ca/diary.html

However, not all women were subject to the strict rigors of society. According to Sir Blackstone, an unmarried woman was considered a *feme sole* and could sign contracts, own a business, control her own wages, buy and/or sell property, and distribute personal property and chattel in her will. A *feme sole* could also sue or be sued in her own name in a court of law. As McKinnon correctly notes, some *feme sole* women were able to establish employment as midwives, newspaper owners, successful seamstresses, tavern keepers, and shopkeepers. Such positions enabled women to work within the accepted sphere of gendered society (and/or sometimes in conjunction with family members, husbands, or business partners) and earn incomes that placed them in the middling ranks. For example, a Mrs. Cumming of Charlestown, South Carolina was a successful loyalist midwife who petitioned the British government for financial assistance following the loss of her business.[105] A Mrs. Griffiths,

---

[105] *American Loyalists, Transcripts of the Manuscript Books and Papers of the Commission of Enquiry into the Losses and Services of the American Loyalist*, IV, 284. From Robert Woodward Barnwell, Jr., "George Harland Hartle'ys Claim for Losses as a Loyalist," *The South Carolina Historical and Genealogical Magazine*, 51, no. 1 (1950): 45-50.

a Connecticut milliner, supported herself and her son prior to the war.[106]

Unfortunately, the status of *feme sole* afforded women the most freedom but was publicly and socially discouraged, since women were viewed as "unproductive" if they were not wedded and having babies.[107]

Mary Fisher,

Has just imported from LONDON, a fresh assortment of WINTER GOODS, which she sells at her shop, just to the northward of the Rev. Mr. CARY's Meeting house, in *Newbury Port*. *Amongst her Goods are,*

A GREAT variety of best double Camblets for riding hoods ; a number of scarlet broad cloths with fur trimmings and snails. Also, Blankets, Duffils, Baizes, Kerseys, Bath Beavers, Ratteens, broad Cloths with suitable Trimmings. With most articles that are wanted for women's or men's wear. Any of which will be sold as cheap as at any shop in town

Essex Journal and Merrimack Packet, Wednesday, June 29th, 1774

One limited way married women were able to assert their rights and control their own businesses interests was to become *feme sole traders*. Typically, deserted women and sailors' wives could petition their

---

[106] Ibid.

[107] If a young woman did not marry, she was expected to live with her brother, or some other married male relative, and help care for his family. The male relative would assume the responsibility of caretaker and provider for the single woman.

colonial legislatures to acquire such status. However, other married women could also achieve this status if their husbands granted permission. The status of feme *sole traders* was understood to mean that married women could conduct business and were responsible for their own actions.[108]

Women in the eighteenth century also acted independently as "deputy husbands", a term coined by historian Laurel Thatcher Ulrich. As a deputy husband, the wife could take over her husband's job or business in his absence. This usually occurred in family businesses such as stores, taverns, mills, and the like. Women were familiar with the business and kept it running smoothly while their husbands were incapacitated or away. The role of deputy husband allowed married women to purchase supplies, pay bills, bank, and perform all other aspects of running their businesses. Likewise, during times of war, women ran their plantations, businesses,

---

[108] The creation of the *femme sole trader* status was motivated by economic, rather than liberal, concerns. In other words, legislatures favored the granting of such status in an effort to keep women and their dependent children off of poor relief programs. War would cause many women to support themselves because their husbands had died or were crippled as a result of their service. During most wars, women remained at home to run farms, plantations, and their families' businesses until the men returned from battle.

farms, families, and managed the servants, while their husbands served in the military. Such was the case during the American Revolution and women, whether Tory or Whig, did whatever was necessary to keep the home front running.

On the eve of the American Revolution, many women found themselves taking on roles inconsistent with their subordinate status within patriarchal households. For example, loyalist women quickly became active participants in the debate over the looming conflict and took their first steps onto the political stage by writing petitions and pamphlets to rebel officials. In one such piece of literature, *A Dialogue Between a Southern Delegate and His Spouse*, a loyalist woman berated her husband, a delegate to the First Continental Congress, and warned of the dire consequences of Congress's actions:

> To your mighty Congress, your members were sent
> To lay our complaints before Parliament,
> Usurpation reared its head from that fatal Hour
> You resolved, you enacted like a Sovereign Power.
> Your non-imports, and Exports are full fraught with Ruin,
> Of thousands and thousands the utter undoing,
> If Philadelphia or New York proposed some wise Plan
> From that moment on you branded the man...

Instead of imploring their Justice or Pity,
You treat Parliament like a Pack of Banditti.
Instead of Addresses fram'd on Truth or on Reason,
You breathe nothing but insult, rebellion and Treason.
In all the Records of the most slavish Nation,
You'll not find an instance of such usurpation,
If spirits infernal for dire vengeance design'd,
Had been named Delegates to afflict humankind,
And in Grand Continental Congress had resolved,
Let the bonds of social bliss be henceforth dissolved.
Oh! My Country! Remember that a woman unknown
Cry'd aloud like Cassandra in Oracular Tone,
Repent! Or you are forever, forever undone.[109]

Some loyalist women even played a military role in the

Revolution. Ann Novil, a Pennsylvania loyalist, acted as a guide during

the 1777 Burgoyne expedition from Canada. Another woman, Frances

Child, helped British and loyalist prisoners escape from New York, while

Hannah Tomlinson "aided and assisted upwards of 100 Prisoners of War

in making their escape into the British lines."[110] Most loyalist women,

however, stayed behind enemy lines and remained within their

communities. While there, they were viewed as a valuable intelligence

---

[109] Mary V. *A Dialogue Between a Southern Delegate and His Spouse*, (New York: 1774). Pamphlet. From https://archive.org/details/southerndele00maryrich.
[110] *Petition of Ann Novil, Frances Child, Hannah Tomlinson.* British Headquarter Papers, document number unavailable. From McKinnon, *While the Women*, 45.

asset by British officials. Women often made better spies than men since their actions were less carefully scrutinized. Likewise, because they could not serve in the militia, hold political office or sign loyalty oaths, women found it easier to avoid accusations of acting as agitators or dissidents.

When loyalist men fled to the safety of British lines, many expressed a belief that their wives and children would be would be spared from the political violence because they were innocent bystanders. From the male perspective, their wives were mere appendages with no independent wills or political roles of their own. Likewise, many male loyalists assumed, under the theories of *feme sole trader* and deputy husbands, that if their spouses were left behind, personal and real property would be carefully protected from seizure or destruction. As Captain Alexander McDonald opined "surely the people [the rebels] has not got so barberously mad as to Mollest or hurt a poor innocent woman and still more Innocent poor Children."[111]

---

[111] Alexander McDonald, *Letters Extracted from the Letter Book of Capt. Alexander McDonell of the Royal Highland Emigrants written from Halifax, Windsor and Cornwallis between the years 1775 and 1779*, 263. Journal. From McKinnon, *While the Women*, 52.

18th Century Woodcut Image, Artist Unknown

Unfortunately, such a view was summarily rejected by the enemy.
Rebel committees and colonial governments concluded that unless there
was evidence to the contrary, the families of fleeing male loyalists shared
in the guilt. From the patriot perspective, women could not act
independently from the men in their lives and thus, the political decisions
of the men also incriminated the women. By joining the enemy and
participating in often vicious raids against frontier communities, the men

had tainted not only themselves but their families as well. Many rebels demanded punishment of those loyalist men who fought against the cause of independence. Unfortunately, these men were in Canada, New York City and other safe havens beyond the rebel's reach. In turn, many Americans directed their attention towards the loyalist women who were left behind and began to see them as vipers living in their midst. Over a short span of time, it was the women and their families who bore the brunt of the rebels' rage.[112]

Women and families that were branded as loyalists were subjected to various forms of punishment, the most common and devastating being the confiscation of their property. Looting and destruction of loyalist property was also an accepted practice. Finally, many women also faced imprisonment and violence at the hand of local mobs.

Loyalist Sarah Mcginnis of New York enjoyed a close relationship with neighboring Mohawks. At the outbreak of the war, New York rebels offered her twelve shillings per day and a guard of fifteen men if she

---

[112] McKinnon, *While the Women*, 42.

would try to influence the Mohawk on their behalf. Instead, she provided intelligence to British authorities and assisted loyalist refugees with their flight north. In retaliation, local patriot officials arrested her son in law and plundered her property. Sarah, her daughter, and her granddaughter watched as rebels sold at public auction all of their possessions, "except what would scantily support them in victuals and clothes." Immediately afterwards, the three women were imprisoned in a local fort and treated so badly that Sarah's granddaughter later died. Sarah and her daughter "escaped at night with only what they could carry on their backs." Tragically, Sarah was forced to leave behind a son "who was out of his senses and bound in chains ... and who some time afterward was burnt alive."[113]

Loyalist Philip Empy was subjected to "many insults and abuses from rebels" and was eventually imprisoned with his three sons in a local jail. When the four escaped, rebels turned their eyes towards his wife and seven remaining children. They were quickly arrested and their property

---

[113] Great Britain Audit Office Records Volume 27. McKinnon, *While the Women*, 68.

confiscated. Mrs Empy and her family were eventually released. But when she returned to her home, she was "beat and abused by 4 men" who left her on the road. Although she was rescued by friends and taken to Schenectady, she later died.[114]

Elizabeth Cary Wilstee was a resident of the New Hampshire Grants whose family had been victimized by the Green Mountain Boys in the 1760s. She watched helplessly as a rebel mob ransacked her home in 1776. In the middle of winter, "the outlaws" again broke into her home and ordered her family to leave. Although it was snowy and cold, she had no other choice. "Looking back while on her way," she saw the "outlaws moving her furniture and provisions from the house and loading them into a wagon." Next she witnessed them "open her feather beds and shake the feathers from the ticks out of the windows and put the ticks and bed clothes into the wagon." Finally, she watched them "pry the logs of the sides of the house out at the corners until the roof fell in." Having finished

---

[114] Philip Empy Petition, March 1, 1780. From Haldimand Papers, Additional Manuscripts No. 21874, folio A776; McKinnon, *While the Women*, 58.

with the Wiltsee home, the mob moved on to the homes of other loyalist tenants in the neighborhood.[115]

Shortly after his escape, Daniel McAlpin's property was seized and his wife and family were arrested. Mary McAlpin described her family's treatment at the hands of the rebels in vivid language:

> From the day her husband left to the day she was forced from her home the Captain's house was never without parties of the Rebels present. They lived at their discretion and sometimes in very large numbers. They destroyed what they could not consume. Shortly after the capture of the fleeing loyalists a group of armed Rebels with blackened faces broke into the McAlpin's dwelling house. They threatened Mary and her children with violence and menace of instant death. They confined them to the kitchen while they stripped every valuable from the home. A few days after this, by an order of the Albany Committee, a detachment of Rebel Forces came and seized upon the remainder of McAlpin's estate both real and personal.[116]

Mary McAlpin and her children were taken to an unheated hut located in Stillwater and locked inside "without fire, table, chairs or any

---

[115] McKinnon, *While the Women,* 56.
[116] *American Loyalists,* 43-47, 54, 51-62

other convenience."[117] Hoping that the hardship would eventually break Mrs. McAlpin and induce her to beg her husband to honorably surrender, the rebels kept Mary and her children in captivity for several weeks. Mary McAlpin refused to comply and instead responded her husband "had already established his honour by a faithful service to his King and country."[118] Enraged, rebels seized Mary and her oldest daughter, stripped both down to their shifts and "carted" both of them through Albany as they were pelted with dirt and rotten vegetables.[119]

As violence, imprisonment and looting continued to mount, many loyalist women recognized their situation was becoming desperate. In a letter to her husband John, Mary Munro described just how dangerous her situation was. "For heavens sake, my dear Mr. Munro, send me some

---

[117] Ibid. On May 27, 1777 General Gates condemned the actions of local militiamen who raided the McAlpin home. However, Gates did little to prevent McAlpin's property from being sold to support the American war effort.

[118] William Smith, *Memoirs of William Smith, May 12, 1777.* Journal.

[119] Great Britain Audit Office Records, Volume 21, reel number B-1159. One local minister later recalled, "Mrs. McAlpin was brought down to Albany in a very scandalous manner so much that the Americans themselves cried out about it." A second account asserted "when Mrs. McAlpin was brought from the hut to Albany as a prisoner with her daughter . . . they neither of them had a rag of cloaths to shift themselves.Eventually, Mary and her children fled to Canada and were reunited with Daniel. Ibid.

relief by the first safe hand. Is there no possibility of your sending for us? If there is no method fallen upon we shall perish, for you can have no idea of our sufferings here; Let me once more intreat you to try every method to save your family; my heart is so full it is ready to break; adieu my Dearest John, may God Almighty bless pre serve and protect you, that we may live to see each other is the constant prayer of your affectionate tho' afflicted wife ... P.S. The Childer's kind love to you."[120] In a second letter, Mary reiterated her desperate situation when she declared, "My dear John I hope when you receive these few lines they may find you in good health. Your Dear Children are all well. As for myself, I am in a poor state of health and very much distresst. I must leave my house in a very short time and God knows where I shall get a place to put my head in, for my own relations are my greatest enemies, the mills they have had a long time in their possession - likewise all their tenants' houses and lands. They have

---

[120] Mary Munro, *Mary Munro to John Munro, undated letter*. Letter. From Haldimand Papers, AddMss A748; McKinnon, *While the Women*, 63.

distresst me beyond expression. I have scarcely a mouthful of bread for myself or children."[121]

Ultimately, many loyalist women concluded they and their families would be safer by withdrawing to British held territory north in Canada or south in New York City.[122] Despite popular misconception, loyalist women and their families generally did not gather their belongings and flee into the night. Instead, many had to appear before local Committees of Safety or similar organizations and request permission to leave the community to join their husbands. Officials carefully scrutinized petitions of loyalist women and set strict terms regarding their departure through an order of removal. In 1780 New York, all women whose husbands were with the enemy were ordered to leave the colony for British bases within twenty days. Patriot committees drew up lists of the women to be removed and officials were designated to inform the women of their fate and of the

---

[121] Mary Munro, *Mary Munro to John Munro, undated letter*, From Haldimand Papers, Add Mss 21,875. McKinnon, *While the Women*, 74.
[122] McKinnon, *While the Women*, 75-76.

consequences of ignoring the order.[123] Women were also subject to severe

restrictions on what they were allowed to take when they departed from

their community. In Vermont, Mrs Jeremiah French was escorted to the

east side of Lake Champlain following her departure from her community.

The notice ordering her removal specified that she could take with her

only "two feather beds and bedding not exceeding Eight Sheets, six

Coverlids or blankets, 5 plates, two platters, two basons, one Quart Cup, &

knives & forks if she has such things, her own & her childrens Wearing

apparril . . . [the rest of the] . . . moveables belonging to sd. Estate . . .

[were to be sold to] Defray the charge of Transportation."[124] When

Loyalist Alida Van Alstine fled to New York City, she was only permitted

to take with her "bedding, 2 Chests, 1 Trunk, 2 bbls. flour, wearing

apparel and some household furniture."[125]

At first, many committees were reluctant to release loyalist

families as they served a useful purpose as hostages. From the rebel

---

[123] McKinnon, *While the Women*, 86.
[124] Vermont Governor and Council, 28 May 1778.
[125] McKinnon, *While the Women*, 86.

perspective, the continued presence of loyalist families under their careful guard could deter future military attacks, stem the flow of young male recruits into Canada or New York City and encourage the release of American prisoners held by British authorities.[126] However, following Burgoyne's invasion of 1777, many local committees recognized that hostages would not prevent future British raids and agreed to release women and their families. Likewise, the decision to allow women and their families to flee was prompted by financial concerns, including a reluctance to care for indigent loyalists. As the Albany County Commissioners for Detecting and Defeating Conspiracies declared in 1778, "it having appeared to us that those Women are become chargeable to the Districts in which they severally reside and that they together with their Families are subsisted at public Expence."[127]

Many states took proactive measures and also passed laws ordering the *expulsion* of loyalist families from their territories. As Burgoyne

---

[126] McKinnon, *While the Women*, 83.

[127] Victor Hugo Palsitis, *Minutes for the Commissioners for Detecting and Defeating Conspiracies in the State of New York, Albany County Sessions, 1778-1781.*, (Albany: J.B. Lyon, 1909), September 21, 1778.

advanced south into New York, the Vermont Council of Safety became alarmed at the military roles loyalist women were assuming. In response, it declared "all such persons as have joined or may hereafter join the British Troops (& left or may hereafter leave) their wives and families within this State, Have their wives and families sent to General John Burgoins [sic] Head Quarters, or some other Branch of the Ministerial Army, as soon as may be."[128] The Albany County Commissioners wrote to the governor of New York in July 1777 asking that "Women whose Husbands are with the Enemy may be sent to the Enemies Lines" and again, in September 1779, requesting the removal of a Mrs Tuttle whose husband, Stephen, "has gone off to the Enemy some time ago."[129]

When loyalists left their communities and traveled north to Canada, they usually followed one of two routes. Loyalists from New York typically followed an overland route through Native American territory to Lake Ontario. Because much of the travel was along forest

---

[128] "Proceedings September 12, 1777". *Records of the Council of Safety,* 166. McKinnon, *While the Women,* 74.
[129] Palsitis, *Minutes for the Commissioner*; September 15, 1779.

trails, Indian guides were essential.[130] Unfortunately for many refugees,

the route included passage through territory held by the Oneidas, an ally of

the Americans. Likewise, refugees had to avoid Continental and militia

detachments that actively patrolled the region. Once clear of enemy

territory, refugees crossed Lake Ontario at Oswego or followed the

southern shore of the lake to the Niagara River.[131] The trip along the

Niagara was often difficult, especially in time of spring floods.

Those refugees from the Hampshire Grants usually followed a

combined land and water route along Lake Champlain and the Richelieu

River to Montreal.[132] The roads followed were often muddy and in poor

condition. Refugees could only use pack horses, ponies, or hand and

horse carts for their belongings and provisions. Securing water

---

[130] Ibid, 89.
[131] Ibid, 87.
[132] Ibid, 88.

transportation was critical to the flight north.[133] Often refugees were often

forced to seek shelter on insect infested or low lying islands in the middle

of Lake Champlain. Because of the difficulties of this combined land and

water passage, loyalists were forced to travel in groups whose members

could share the burden of carrying boats and provisions.[134]

Some loyalists might be lucky enough to make the trip in thirteen

days, but most took much longer. An expedition of women and children

that had to move slowly, was not lucky enough to make good connections

with boats, and experienced bad weather could take from two to three

months to reach the Quebec Province.[135] The delay in travel, combined

with the rugged country took its toll on the clothing of loyalist women and

---

[133] Those loyalists who failed to secure boats often found themselves trapped in the Hampshire Grants.

[134] It was not uncommon for loyalists travelling from the Hampshire Grants to pass through villages and towns devastated by war and battlefields littered with the decomposing bodies of British and American dead.

[135] Ibid, 89.

children.[136] It was not uncommon for refugees to exhaust their supplies and be forced to survive on nuts, roots and leaves.[137]

The experience of loyalist Mary Munro highlights the hardships loyalist women encountered during the Revolutionary War. Munro had been forced to flee from her home in Shaftsbury, Hampshire Grants to Canada following the defeat of Burgoyne. As they traveled towards Lake George to join others en route to Canada, they lightened their load by discarding food and "most of their wearing Apparel. . . After much difficulty, [they] arrived at Lake George and . . .lay in the woods Six days almost perished with Cold and Hunger . . . until three other families arrived. . . [afterwards they] prevailed on the commanding officer at Fort Edward to give them a boat and a flag, they set off across Lake

---

[136] Henry Watson Powell, *Powell to Haldimand, July 10, 1779*. Letter. From Haldimand Papers, AddMss 21,793. According to Cartwright, "the wet Weather, the Badness of the Roads, and the various Difficulties of so long a Journey, at this late season of the Year which seemed at once to encounter me, were sufficient to discourage one who had scarce ever been from Home before. But the Prospect before me of pursuing my original Plan of Life, and enjoying Peace with all its attendant Blessings made me look upon the Fatigues of the Way as Trifles. When travelling through the Wet and Dirt, I would say to myself by way of comfort this will make a fair Day and good Roads the more agreeable. And indeed we should not know the Value of good Things did we not sometimes experience their contrary Evils." Richard Cartwright Jr. *A Journey to Canada, c. 1777*. Journal. From http://www.62ndregiment.org/A_Journey_to_Canada_by_Cartwright.pdf
[137] McKinnon, *While the Women*, 89-90.

George."[138]   Unfortunately for Mary, they were "discovered by a party of Indians from Canada - which pursued them. . . as a result of the excessive hardships they underwent," Mary and her children were "very sickly the whole Winter" after arriving in Canada. The toll the journey took on Mary was sadly announced by her husband when he declared "the children recovered [from their illnesses] but Mrs. Munro never will."[139]

[138] John Munro, *Memorial of Captain John Munro*, John Munro Papers, AO. McKinnon, *While the Women*, 92.

[139] Ibid

Chapter Seven: "Come Gentlemen Tories, Firm, Loyal and True" [140]

When General Burgoyne's and his army departed southward from

Canada towards the American Colonies, Jessup's Corps advanced south

and joined the expedition at Fort St. John's. Evidence suggests the unit

was ordered to serve with General Fraser's Advanced Corps and was

assigned as an advance party on the left flank.[141] It is likely the corps was

utilized as scouts and foragers and were charged with the tasks of securing

food, horses, wagons and cattle from the surrounding countryside. Of

---

[140] "Come gentlemen Tories, firm loyal and true. Here are axes and shovels and something to do!" Frank Moore, *Songs and Ballads of the American Revolution* (New York, 1856), 259.

[141] "Brigadier Fraser had already moved ahead with his brigade and the Canadian Companies of Monin and Boucherville, as well as with the detachment of [Captain] Fraser and a considerable corps of Savages. The Provincial corps of Peters and Jessup had also gone on." Johann Friedrich Specht, *The Specht Journal,* June 18, 1777. Journal; In September Specht would state "Unlike the corps of Savages and the Canadian Companies of Boucherville and Monin, the Provincial corps of Peters and Jessup, as well as the corps of Captain Fraser advanced father to give the left wing of the army greater security." Ibid, September 14, 1777.

course, as Burgoyne advanced further south, elements of Jessup's Corps were utilized in early operations against American forces stationed in and around Ticonderoga.

On July 2, 1777, a large force under the command of Captain Alexander Fraser of the Select Marksmen successfully secured Mount Hope, a rise located north of the American lines. That same day, Fraser dispatched his marksmen, Native Americans and Jessup's Corps to cut off American forces attempting to retire from Mount Hope to Ticonderoga. Unfortunately, as Burgoyne described "The Indians . . . attacked too soon . . . and the Enemy were thereby able to retire with the loss of one officer and a few men killed and one officer wounded."[142] Nevertheless,

---

[142] Burgoyne Papers, July 2, 1777; Anburey, Travels America, 1: 318; Stone, Memoirs Riedesel, 1: 110-112; S. Sydney Bradford. ed., "Lord Francis Napier's Journal of the Burgoyne Campaign." Mayland Historical Magazine Volume 57, Baltimore (#4 Dec. 1962) p. 298. Napier states that the casualties suffered by Captain Fraser's pursuit party were as follows: Lieutenant Houghton, 2 privates of the Marksmen (both from the 62nd Regiment), 1 private of Jessup's unit and 3 Indians wounded. In addition 1 Indian was killed and a1 private of the Marksmen (from the 47th Regiment) taken prisoner; Stevens, Facsimilies of Manuscripts. Document # 1571 pp. 7-8 Letter from Brigadier General Simon Fraser to John Robinson July 13th 1777 for confirmation of Captain Fraser's movements and casualties on July 2nd; For an American notation of action see William B. Weeden, ed., "Diary of Enos Hitchcock," in Rhode Island Historical Society Publications Volume 7. (Providence (1899)), 116.

Burgoyne correctly noted that the operation successfully cut the enemy "off from communication with Lake George."[143]

A View of Ticonderoga from a Point on the North Shore of Lake Champlain by James Hunter, 1774

The next day, Burgoyne dispatched Jessup's corps, as well as a contingent of British troops and Native American warriors, to the eastern shore of Lake Champlain.[144] For the next three days the contingent

---

[143] Burgoyne Papers, July 2, 1777.

[144] The Native Americans who were aiding Burgoyne occasionally failed to distinguish Loyalist from Patriot. On July 26, 1777 in a bloody surprise attack, they raided the Hampshire Grants farm of John Allen, a loyalist sympathizer, and brutally killed him, his wife, their three small children, his sister-in-law, and two slaves. Their house afterward

launched a series of raids against American settlements near Otter Creek, located east-northeast of Crown Point. The operation had little effect on the American populace and no influence on the military operations against Fort Ticonderoga, Mount Independence or Hubbardton.[145] By July 10, 1777, Jessup's rejoined Burgoyne's army at Skenesboro.

After much delay, on July 22, 1777, Burgoyne resumed his advance south towards Fort Anne. The army, now moving at a considerably slower pace, arrived at the fort on July 24th. On July 26th, the army moved on Kingsboro, located two miles north of Fort Edward. Four days later, Jessup's was once again with Captain Fraser's detachment and was located one mile south of the fort and conducting operations against nearby rebel forces.

"presented a horrid spectacle." The next day, near Fort Edward, Indians captured, killed, and scalped a young woman named Jane McCrea, who was betrothed to a loyalist officer in Jessup's Corps. The story of Jane McCrea later became symbolic of the chaos of Burgoyne's campaign; the Allen family tragedy, on the other hand, has largely been forgotten. See also *The Specht Journal,* July 3, 1777 for a description of operations around Fort Ticonderoga on July 3rd.

[145] Although secondary sources assert Jessup's was present at the Battle of Hubbardton, no primary source exists confirming that the unit was present at this engagement. Instead, evidence suggests that the corps was still attached to Alexander Fraser's Select Marksmen and was in the Otter Creek region conducting raids when the Battle of Hubbardton took place.

30th July we remov'd to the height one mile on the other side Fort Edward near the Road leading to Albany, the Rebels advanc'd post one mile in our front. Same evening the Indians, and Jessop's Corps of American Volunteers, attack'd their advanc'd post, and drove them on the other side of Hudson's River with the loss of one Man only. Same Night the whole Rebel Army retreated; such is the natural bravery of our Indians, for they know nothing of the Art of War, they put their Arms into a Canoe, and swim over the River, pushing the Canoe before them, and many of them carried their Fuzees in their mouths, with their powder horns ty'd upon their Heads.

3rd August a party of Indians and American Volunteers, went on a Scout, they fell in with an advanc'd Guard of the Rebels, consisting of three hundred Men (under the command of a Major), at sunrise on the 4th the Rebels were defeated with the loss of four kill'd (amongst whom was the Major) and seven Prisoners; same Day another party of our Indians defeated a body of the Rebels and kill'd eleven of them.[146]

Meanwhile, on July 30, 1777, General Fraser dispatched a party of Native Americans to locate and escort Daniel McAlpin and his recruits safely into camp. Over the next few days, other Tories, including William Fraser and his men, also trickled in, "wishing to serve either for the

[146] *Diary of Joshua Pell Jr.,* July 30, 1777 and August 3, 1777; John Austin Stevens. "Diary of Joshua Pell, Junior an Officer of the British Army in America 1776 - 1777." *The Magazine of American History with Notes and Queries,* February 1878.

duration of the campaign or until the end of the war."[147] As one observer

noted "they came as they could, some from prisons, and some from

committees . . . naked and barefoot, but with good hearts; no money being

given to clothe them."[148]

According to period accounts, only one third of the loyalists

joining Burgoyne at Fort Edward were properly armed and equipped.[149]

As the general noted "[some] hundreds of men, a third part of them with

arms, have joined me since I have penetrated this place, professing

themselves loyalists, and wishing to serve, some to the end of the war,

some for the campaign. Though I am without instructions upon this

subject, I have not hesitated to receive them, and as fast as companies can

be formed, I shall post the officers till a decision can be made upon the

---

[147] John Burgoyne, *Burgoyne to Germaine, July 11, 1777.* Letter; John Burgoyne, *A State of the Expedition from Canada as Laid Before the House of Commons*, (London, 1780), Appendix xxxvii. "Between 30 and 60 daily entered headquarters to take another loyalty oath and quite a few of them decided to take up arms together with us for the general good." *The Specht Journal*, August 21, 1777. The German officer further noted on August 23rd "Almost all the Savages have returned via Fort George to Canada by now so that Brigadier Fraser did not retain many more than 50. His corps of Provincials, on the other hand, increases daily." Ibid, August 23, 1777.
[148] Haldimand to Colonel John Peters, October 27, 1780.
[149] Hadden, *Journal and Orderly Books*, 71.

measure by my superiori. I mean to employ them particularly upon detachments, for keeping the country in awe, and procuring cattle, their real use I expect will be great in the preservation of the national troops: but the impression which will be caused upon public opinion."[150]

Of course, Burgoyne moved to arm and supply these volunteers as quickly as possible.[151] Because the general did not bring military weapons for incoming Loyalist recruits, it is likely these men were armed with civilian muskets seized from the local populace or taken from incoming refugees. For example, on September 7, 1777, sixteen civilian arms were delivered to McAlpin's Corps. As subsequent correspondence noted, "Some days ago the General told me there were a dozen firelocks at Head Quarters, which would arm so many of the provincials; you will have the goodness to give directions for delivering them to the bearer a Serjeant of

---

[150] John Burgoyne, *Burgoyne to Lord Germain, July 11, 1777*. Letter.

[151] Many of the loyalists were immediately assigned to field and logistical operations. According to Specht, "All the regiments of the line had to provide 1 officer and 25 men today to restore the road between here and Fort George. A number of well-affected Provincials also joined in this work. Under the direction of Governor Skene, an office was established at headquarters by respectable and loyal Provincials to regulate all such matters which concerned the local inhabitants, the deserters of the Rebels, the recruitment, commerce and sale of horses and cattle; moreover, all those that were looking for protection." *The Specht Journal*, August 6, 1777.

Captain Macalpins Corps. I am Dr. Sir your most obedient humble Servant Sm Fraser...Sept. 7th 1777; Head Quarters. Recd. Sixteen firelocks (that were brought in by Inhabitants to the Commissioners) for the use of Capt. Macalpins Corps. Thos Fraser Lieut. in Captn. McAlpin Corps."[152]

Captain Hugh Munro's Bateaux Company

Hugh Munro was a prosperous saw mill owner who owned property on the Upper Hudson. When war broke out, Munro actively recruited over a dozen men on behalf of his neighbor Ebenezer Jessup.[153] Munro initially served under Jessup's command, however, when it was deemed necessary to transport critical supplies from Canada via water routes, he was awarded command of a bateaux company. Men were drawn from Jessup's Corps as well as recruited from the local Tory population to fill the ranks of the bateaux company.

Following the company's creation, Munro and his men were

---

[152] GLC 4764.35, Gilder Lehrman Collection, On Deposit at the New-York Historical Society.

[153] Payroll of Captain Hugh Munro's Company, July 13, 1777 to August 8, 1777.

placed under Jessup's supervision. However, circumstances changed very rapidly. While the British army rested at Fort Edward, General Fraser assisted McAlpin with the organization of his own corps of volunteers, known as McAlpin's Corps of American Volunteers.[154] Recognizing the unit was significantly short of recruits, Fraser first ordered forty-two of the original fifty-six men recruited by McAlpin and enrolled in Jessup's Corps to be transferred back to McAlpin's command. These men were drawn from Captains Edward Jessup, Jonathan Jones and Joseph Jessup's Companies.[155] Naturally, Ebenezer Jessup objected to this decision.[156]

On August 16, 1777, the general ordered Munro and his men to be reassigned to McAlpin's Corps. Fraser also established a pay scale and authorized McAlpin to utilize the men as he saw fit.[157] Ebenezer Jessup

---

[154] It appears that during the Burgoyne campaign, McAlpin's Corps was also known as "Voluntiers under the Command of Daniel McAlpin".

[155] Sixteen men were drawn from Captain Edward Jessup's Company. Six were drawn from Captain Jonathan Jones' Company. Twenty- two men were drawn from Captain Joseph Jessup's Company.

[156] See Memorial of Ebenezer Jessup, February 1, 1778. Over the next few years, Jessup would repeatedly complain to Haldimand about the transfer of men from his corps to McAlpin's.

[157] Simon Fraser, *A True Copy, of the Establishment for a Company of Batteau Men to be formed from the Men engaged by Captn. McALPIN, of the Royal Americans August 16,*

became enraged and repeatedly protested to the transfer.[158] Likewise, Captain Munro protested the reassignment and refused to let his company muster with McAlpin's Corps.[159] However, McAlpin quickly moved to limit the men's influence over his newly acquired bateaux company. The loyalist leader swelled the bateaux company's ranks and officer corps with his own men to ensure the unit would remain loyal to him. In the end, McAlpin emerged victorious in the internal conflict.

Understandably, Jessup's objections had less to do with the loss of men than the loss of potential officer commissions. As Burgoyne reflected "[Jessup's and Peter's] battalions are now in embryo . . . Sir Guy Carleton has given me blank commissions for the officers, to fill up occasionally, and the agreement with them is, that the commissions are not to be so

1777. Order. Great Britain, British Library, Additional Manuscripts, No. 21827, folio 122. As Fraser ordered, "The Officers to have British Pay, the Non-commisioned Officers to have three Shillings Halifax Currency and the Privates to have Two shillings Halifax per Day, Captn. McALPIN will find fit Men to be employ'd on this Service, and is hereby authorised to engage them according to the Conditions above specefied."

[158] Ebenezer Jessup, *Ebenezer Jessup to Lemaistre, February 1, 1778.* Letter.

[159] Hugh Munro, *Hugh Munro to Haldimand, September 12, 1780.* Letter.

effective, till two thirds of the battalions are raised."[160] Thus, if Jessup

was unable to to keep his troops, he would be unable to secure coveted

commissions from Burgoyne. In turn, he and his officers would only

receive minimal pay and would not receive the full benefits established for

men of their respective ranks.

Regardless of the dispute, the bateaux company was responsible

for transporting supplies from Fort Edward to Burgoyne's army while

under the protection of McAlpin's Volunteers. Barrels of pork and flour

were shipped down Lakes Champlain and George to the fort. In turn,

Munro's men transported the maggot infested casks to Fort Miller where

the supplies were carried overland to Burgoyne. The task was excessively

difficult and dangerous. According to Charles Carroll, the "current is

exceedingly rapid. Some places the bateau men were obliged to set up

with poles and drag the boat by the painter . . . sometimes for whole days

up to the waist in water or mire."[161] Complicating matters, rebel patrols

continuously attacked the convoy and attempted to seize boats in an effort

---

[160] Burgoyne, *Burgoyne to Lord Germain, July 11, 1777.*
[161] Fraser, *Skulking* at 48.

114

to disrupt the supply line. No less than seven of McAlpin's men were captured during the month of August.[162]

By the beginning of September, Munro's Company had delivered a month's supply of food and provisions to the army. In turn, Burgoyne's forces resumed its march southward. Munro's bateaux company was ordered to shadow the Hessians as they advanced down a road adjacent to the Hudson River. The remainder of McAlpin's Corps was assigned to the advanced corps under the command of General Fraser.[163]

---

[162] Ibid at 128-132. See also Ebenezer Jessup, *Ebenezer Jessup to General John Burgoyne, 1778.* Letter.

[163] Eric Schnitzer, *Organization of the Army from Canada commanded by Lieutenant General John Burgoyne, September 19 to October 7, 1777.* It should be noted that Burgoyne referred to McAlpin's Corps as "Voluntiers under the Command of Daniel McAlpin." Ibid.

Plan of the Position Which the Army under Lt. Gen. Burgoyne Took at Saratoga, Author Unknown, 1777

On September 10, 1777 McAlpin's Corps of American Volunteers and the Advance Corps were located east of the Town of Saratoga and the ruins of Fort Hardy while Burgoyne's forces were located to the southwest. Over the next several days McAlpin's Corps engaged in a series of probing and foraging operations between Sword and Freeman's Farms.

The First Battle of Freeman's Farm

At the outset of the battle, McAlpin's advanced with General Fraser and his corps towards Freeman's Farm. When Burgoyne engaged

116

the enemy, McAlpin's and the other loyalist units under the Fraser's command were deployed south of the battle line and held in reserve. At some point during the ensuing battle, McAlpin's was brought forward to engage the enemy. As the fighting raged, Lieutenant Peter Drummond was captured.[164] According to a memorial letter from McAlpin to General Haldimand, "Capt. Drummond had the Misfortune to be taken prisoner in the field of Battle on the 19th Septr 1777 when he was exerting himself in

---

[164] Daniel McAlpin, *Memorial of Captain Daniel McAlpin, November 18, 1778.* Memorial Letter. The full text of the Memorial reads as follows: "To His Excellency Frederick Haldimand, Esq. Governor General of Canada and Territories thereon depending General and Commander in Chief of all His Majesty's Forces therein, etc. The Memorial of Captain Daniel McAlpin of the 60th Regiment humbly sheweth Your Excellency's Memorialist having in concert with Lieutenant Colonel William Edmonston of the 48th Regiment proposed a plan for raising a battalion of his Majesty's loyal subjects in Albany and in the neighbouring counties. Such plan was laid before General Sir William Howe and His Excellency was pleased to approve of the same and he gave this instruction to engage the men, taking care not to appoint more than one captain, two subalterns, three sergeants, three corporals, and one drummer to every 50 men. In consequence of General Howe's instructions your Excellency's Memorialist employed proper people at a considerable expense to engage volunteers for this service and he was so successful that in six months' time five hundred and seventy-two men were engaged, two hundred of which number joined General Burgoyne's army as will appear by a certificate signed by the Deputy Commissary of Musters. Your Excellency's Memorialist did appoint Mr. Peter Drumond to be captain of a company and several other good men to be subalterns. Captain Drummond had the misfortune to be taken prisoner in the field of battle on the 19th September 1777 when he was exerting himself in the execution of his duty and he has since suffered much, being a long time confined in irons in a dungeon. As your Excellency's Memorialist did not appoint but one captain, five lieutenants, five ensigns, and one quarter master to the above number of men he humbly hopes that your Excellency will be good enough to support them in those different stations as they have sacrificed all they had for their loyalty."

the Execution of his duty & he has Since Sufferd much being a long time Confined in Irons in a dungeon."[165]

At the conclusion of the battle, McAlpin's and the other loyalist units retreated southwest from Freeman's Farm to a ridge overlooking the battlefield. British light infantry soldiers formed a protective screen before them while Canadian volunteers set up a post along the loyalist's right flank.

As a result of casualties sustained at the First Battle of Freeman's Farm, many British regular regiments experienced a decrease in combat strength.

To rebuild his regiments, General Burgoyne ordered the loyalist units under his command to draft a percentage of its men and turn them over to these depleted units. Specifically, "one hundred and twenty brave men of courage and fidelity, from the provincial corps of Jessup, Peters, M'Alpin and M'Kay, are to be incorporated, for this campaign only, into the six British regiments, in the proportion of twenty to a regiment. They will have a certificate from under the hand of the Lieutenant-general, to entitle

---

[165] McAlpin to Haldimand, November 18, 1778. It is unknown at this time the number of casualties McAlpin's sustained during the engagement at Freeman's Farm.

them to a discharge on the 25th day of December next. They will besides receive a gratuity on being incorporated, and another at the expiration of their service: and these will be the whole number required this campaign. Those corps, whose establishment is to take place on a certain number of men being raised, are allowed to recommend those furnished upon this occasion as part of that number."[166] Following Burgoyne's orders, many of the men from McAlpin's Corps were drafted into 9th, 20th, 21st, 24th, 47th and 62nd regiments. Although it is possible the loyalist drafts were issued updated arms and equipment, they were never issued regimental

---

[166] John Burgoyne, *Supplement to the State of the Expedition from Canada*, (London, 1780); *The Specht Journal*, September 21, 1777.

clothing.[167]

Return of Provisions Issued to Capt. McAlpins Corps of Volunteers betwixt 1st Septr. & 24th 1777.

| Drawn | | No. Days | No. men | Flour Pds. | Bread Pds. | Fresh Beeff Pds. | Salt Beeff Pds. | Pork | | No. |
from what Time	to What Time							Pds.	Oz.	Rations
1st Septr.	7 Septr.	7	65	679½				284		455
7 Do	9 Do	3	62	279				116	4	186
6 Do	9 Do	4	17	102				42	8	68
10 Do	13 Do	4	89	534				222	8	356
14 Do	17 Do	4	87	522				217	8	348
18 Do	21 Do	4	105	636				265		424
22 Do	23 Do	2	123	359				153	4	246
24 Do		1	100	150				62	8	100
				3261¼				1363	8	2183
25th Do		1	100	150				62	8	100
26 Do	27	2	100	300				125		200
28 Do	29	2	96	288				120		192
30 Do	1 October	2	96	144	144			120		192
2nd October		1	84	126				52	8	84
3 Do		1	84		126			52	8	84
4 Do	to the 8th	4	84	336				210		336

Deerfield Massachusetts, Pocumtuck Valley Memorial Association Library, Revolutionary War, Box 6, folder 16.

In the days that followed the battle, the weather turned cold. As a result, Burgoyne ordered winter gear be prepared for his men. On September 25, 1777 McAlpin's Corps was paid £338 for the purchase of multiple items, including 168 blankets to make capotes, material for 168 cloth leggings, thread, 133 pairs of shoes, 168 "head coverings" and 164 pairs of mittens.[168]

---

[167] Interview with Eric Schnitzer, Saratoga National Historic Park.

[168] Haldimand Papers, manuscript number 21,874, footnote 12; Anbury, *Travels Through the Interior.*

On the eve of the 2nd Battle of Freeman's Farm, many of McAlpin's men remained with Fraser's advanced corps and were relegated to fatigue duty and assisting in the construction of Balcarres Redoubt. Upon its completion, the fortification was "at least one hundred fifty chains [in length]. The walls in some places were six feet high. Eight cannons . . . were mounted in embrasures."[169] The unit was also charged with the responsibility of protecting the bateaux and supply line along the Hudson River.[170]

However, a select number of McAlpin's men were chosen for a much more dangerous mission. According to Sergeant Joseph Beaty, he and other members of the American Volunteers were ordered to infiltrate the American lines "in order to conniture the works and know what number of cannon and how supplied with provisions."[171] The men

---

[169] Captain Pausch, *Pausch to Baurmeister, November 26, 1777.* Letter.

[170] Fraser, *Skulking* at 49. It should be noted Specht states "To protect the train and the baggage, the Hesse-Hanau Regt. remained in its former position, just as the 47th Regt. did with the Provincial Corps under Peters and Jessup at the Hudson to cover the supplies and bateaux." The Specht Journal, September 20, 1777. Francis Clereke's *A View of the West Bank on the Hudson's River . . . (Shewing General Fraser's Funeral)"* depicts Munro's boats moored below the British camp along the banks of the Hudson River.

[171] Joseph Beaty, *Memorial of Ensign Joseph Beaty, October 2, 1781.* Memorial Letter.

successfully entered into the American camp and secured vital intelligence by interviewing an unsuspecting American officer.[172] Afterwards, Beaty travelled to New Scotland, located twelve miles west of Albany and successfully rescued over a dozen loyalist officers, men and civilians.[173]

On October 4, 1777, the sergeant was dispatched by General Fraser to the Hudson River to determine whether British reinforcements under Clinton or Pigot were marching or sailing north to aid Burgoyne. Beaty was able to avoid rebel patrols and travelled over sixty miles south to Catskill, New York. Upon learning no relief was on its way, he returned to General Burgoyne and reported his findings.[174] On October 16, 1777, the sergeant was ordered to travel to New York City to deliver correspondence from Burgoyne to General Clinton pleading for help. Beaty reached New York City on October 21, 1777 and personally delivered the letter to Clinton.[175] By then, it was too late.

---

[172] Ibid.

[173] Ibid. The party arrived back at the British lines on October 3, 1777.

[174] Ibid.

[175] Ibid. Beaty continued his service to the Crown, but was captured by American forces in 1779 and condemned to death in 1780. However, he was rescued and delivered to

122

The British army was exhausted and quickly deteriorating. "The army has become quite fatigued because it had to move out every morning one hour before dawn and stand so long to arms until the fog had completely lifted, which rarely happened before 9 o'clock in the morning. . . The sick and wounded of whom the army had more than 700 had to make do with living in the tents . . . many of them died every day."[176] Supply shortages and price increases became commonplace. "Everything became more expensive from day to day, and many such items as sugar, coffee, tea could no longer be had at all. One quart of rum had now to be paid with 8 shillings . . . a soldier could therefore no longer afford this drink. It was a great relief for the soldiers that every day spruce beer was brewed for them, to which they had already become accustomed."[177]

Canada that same year. Beaty immediately enlisted in Roger's Corps. In 1782, he was captured again and subsequently executed. Prior to his death, Beaty gave a full confession to his captors.

[176] *The Specht Journal*, October 1, 1777.
[177] Ibid.

The Second Battle of Freeman's Farm

It is likely McAlpin's Corps participated in the October 7, 1777 battle against General Horatio Gates' forces. According to Joshua Pell Jr., a volunteer with the 24th Regiment of Foot, the "Canadian Volunteers and Provincials" joined Fraser in a probing expedition and "form'd the column of the left marching thro the wood, where the engagement of 19 September was fought."[178] John F. Luzader, author of *Saratoga: A Military History of the Decisive Campaign of the American Revolution*, indirectly suggests that the loyalists assigned to Fraser's advanced corps, including McAlpin's, accompanied him on the probe and may have engaged elements of Poor's New Hampshire Brigade southwest of the Balcarres Redoubt during the opening shots of the battle.[179]

---

[178] Stevens, *Diary of Joshua Pell*, 110-11.

[179] John F. Luzader, *Saratoga: A Military History of the Decisive Campaign of the American Revolution*, (New York, 2008), 281-285. I am unsure to what extent McAlpin's allegedly participated in the skirmish between Morgan, Poor and Fraser, especially in light of the fact McAlpin's Corps did not sustain any casualties nor are there any claims for compensation for military property lost or damaged as a result of the engagement.

During the thirty minute engagement that followed, Fraser was mortally wounded and his troops were overwhelmed by a combined force of Morgan's riflemen and Poor's Brigade. Desperate, the British and provincial troops retreated back to the safety of Balcarres' and Breymann's Redoubts.[180] In a stroke of ill fortune, some loyalists took refuge in the German occupied Breymann's Redoubt. Once inside the perceived safety of the fortification, McAlpin's and the other units took up a position to the right of the German line.

Despite several direct assaults by Continental troops and extensive hand to hand combat, the Americans failed to capture the Balcarres Redoubt.[181] However, under the direction of General Benedict Arnold, the Americans turned their attention towards Breymann's Redoubt. Despite stiff resistance offered by the German and Loyalist troops, the fortification was quickly overwhelmed. McAlpin and his men evacuated their posts and withdrew southwards towards the Hudson River.

---

[180] Ibid. "The Provincials and Canadians taking part in this affair ran along into the redoubt of Fraser's corps instead of reoccupying the post assigned to them." *The Specht Journal*, October 7, 1777.
[181] Ibid.

A View of the West Bank on the Hudson's River . . . (Shewing General Fraser's Funeral)
by Francis Clereke, 1777

The fall of Breymann's Redoubt would ultimately lead to

Burgoyne's defeat in the Second Battle of Freeman's Farm. In turn, the

general reluctantly concluded his expedition would never reach Albany

nor would reinforcements arrive from General Howe. On the evening of

October 8, 1777, Burgoyne ordered his army to withdraw. As the army

pulled back, the 47th Regiment, Royal Artillery and several loyalist units,

including McAlpin's Corps, remained behind to cover the retreat.[182] By

[182] Gavin Watt, *The British Campaign of 1777: Volume Two The Burgoyne Expedition Burgoyne's Native and Loyalist Auxiliaries*, (Milton, Ontario, Canada: Global Heritage Press, 2013), 53.

dawn, the British army had removed to a nearby hill along the Hudson River. The retreat to Canada had begun.

Chapter Eight: McAlpin's Race to Canada

On October 8, 1777, Captain Munro was ordered to collect the

army's provisions and follow the retreat via the Hudson River.

Unfortunately for Munro, his bateaux company quickly became the rebel's

prime target.[183] According to one rebel, "a few bateaux and scows were

passing along as I arrived . . . they were loaded with military stores, the

baggage of the officers and the women who followed (the British army).

A few well-directed shots brought them to the bank. A rush took place for

the prey. Everything was hauled out and carried back into a low swampy

place in the rear and a guard placed over it . . . the poor females, trembling

in fear, were released and permitted to go in a boat to the British army, a

short distance above on the other side of the river . . . such a group of

---

[183] One American officer who participated in operations against Burgoyne's watercraft was Major Nathan Good, a Stockbridge Indian. A monument to his service asserts: "To commemorate the service of **Major Nathan Goodale,** Oct. 11, 1777. He bravely captured Burgoyne's store boats in the face of the enemy at the mouth of the Fishkill. Under orders of General Gates with 7 scouts he captured 129 prisoners before October 7th. Distinguished services also in 1778. Erected by Emma Jones his great-Grand-Daughter."

tanned and leather visages were never seen before . . . poorly clad . . . and

their persons war-torn and weary."[184]

In response to the repeated attacks on Munro's watercraft,

McAlpin and Jessups' Corps were ordered on October 9, 1777 to attack an

American post located near Saratoga Creek. According to Ebenezer

Jessup:

> I had the honour to command the Party that retook the 18 Batteaux
> and scows of provisions etc. from the enemy near Saratoga Crick
> and ordered Major [Edward]
>
> Jessup with a part of the corps to ford the River to the Island under
> whose cover they were brought up the Crick, with the remainder of
> the Corps I brought up the rear covering the Whole & was ordered
> to the Barracks from whence we were ordered to take post on the
> High Ground . . . Captain McAlpin left the ground between us and
> the Germans that afternoon & the 47th Reg't being recalled that
> night there was not a man but ourselves above the German lines
> Which you thought proper to order us into Camp as soon as it
> came to your knowledge.[185]

Despite the success of the raid, the bateaux were attacked the

following day. As the convoy approached a narrow straight in the

---

[184] John P. Backer, *Sexagenary or Reminiscences of the American Revolution*, (Albany, 1833), 102.

[185] Ebenezer Jessup to General Burgoyne, July 17, 1778. The "barracks" Jessup is referring to is part of an unknown American fortification located near Saratoga Creek.

Hudson, rebels lined the shores and fired upon the boats. In the heat of the battle, Captain Munro was wounded and "fifty bateaux loaded with provisions, stores and medicines, among which were 1000 barrels of pork and beef" were captured.[186]

The next day, the boatmen were forced to transfer the remaining barrels of flour and pork into carts and deliver them overland to the Burgoyne's forces in Saratoga. As the loyalists struggled to unload the boats, American detachments kept up a constant fire. As the day progressed, the rebels brought up an artillery piece and opened fire on the bateaux and its men. Ultimately, the loyalists were forced to seek shelter behind Schuyler Island on the Hudson River.

As the days passed, circumstances were becoming desperate for the loyalist men and women attached to Burgoyne's army. Johann Specht

---

[186] James Thatcher, *Military Journal of the American Revolution*, (Hartford: 1862), 104. Two days later, Ebenezer Jessup led a daring raid and recaptured some of the bateaux near the mouth of Saratoga Creek.

noted living conditions were sparse. "Here and there, little kitchens and boarding huts were built."[187] Refugee Elizabeth Munro Fischer recalled:

> We retreated after the last battle to Saratoga, where we encamped a small distance from the river, to prevent their cannon having any command over us—having nothing to do, waiting General Burgoyne's orders. We were deprived of all comforts of life, and did not dare to kindle fire for fear we should be observed from the other side of the river, and they might fire on us, which they did several times. Being about the middle of October, we suffered cold and hunger; many a day I had nothing but a piece of raw salt pork, a biscuit, and a drink of water—poor living for a nurse. At this time I had my child at my breast, being eleven months old. One day, wearied of living in this manner, I told some of the soldiers' wives if they would join me, I would find out a way to get some provision cooked—seven of them joined me. I spoke to some of the soldiers that were invalid, and told them if they would make up a fire back in the woods, and get a large kettle hung on, we would fill it with provision, and cook it, which would last us some time. They consented to do it for a guinea ; they went to work and built up the fire, hung on the kettle, and put water in it, then we women put in what we pleased ; we soon filled it with a variety ; it began to boil ; we all kept a distance from the fire for fear of the cannon that were placed on the other side of the river on a high hill ; they soon discovered our fire, and saluted us with a cannon ball ; it struck and broke our kettle to pieces, and sent the provision in the air. We met with no hurt only losing our intended feast. The soldiers demanded their pay, which I paid; but as the disappointment was so great, the rest declined paying anything,

---

[187] *The Specht Journal,* October 5, 1777.

saying they had lost enough by losing their provision, so for my folly I had to pay for all.[188]

---

[188] Elizabeth Munro Fischer, *Memoirs of Mrs. Elizabeth Fischer*, (New York, 1810), 13-19. An excellent account of the plight of Burgoyne's Army on the eve of surrender is described by the Baroness von Riedesel.

"October 10, 1777 The whole army clamored for a retreat, and my husband promised to make it possible, provided only that no time was lost But General Burgoyne, to whom an order had been promised if he brought about & junction with the army of General Howe, could not determine upon this course, and lost everything by his loitering. About two o'clock in the afternoon, the firing of cannon and small arms was again heard, and all was alarm and confusion. My husband sent me a message telling me to betake myself forthwith into a house which was not far from there. I seated myself in the calash with my children, and had scarcely driven up to the house, when I saw on the opposite side of the Hudson river, five or six men with guns, which were aimed at us. Almost involuntarily I threw the children on the bottom of the calash and myself over them. At the same instant the churls fired, and shattered the arm of a poor English soldier behind us. Who was already wounded, and was also of the point of retreating into the house.

October 13, 1777 Our cook saw to our meals, but we were in want of water; and in order to quench thirst, I was often obliged to drink wine, and give it, also, to the children. It was, moreover, the only thing that my husband could take, which fact so worked upon our faithful- Rockel, that he said to me one day, "I fear that the General drinks so much wine, because he dreads falling into captivity, and is therefore weary of life." The continual danger in which my husband was encompassed, was a constant source of anxiety to me. I was the only one of all the women, whose husband had not been killed or wounded, and I often said to myself—especially since my husband was placed in such great danger day and night— "Shall I be the only fortunate one?" He never came into the tent at night; but lay outside by the watch fires. This alone was sufficient to have caused his death, as the nights were damp and cold.

October 15, 1777 In this horrible situation we remained six days. Finally, they spoke of capitulating, as by temporizing for so long a time, our retreat had been cut off. A cessation of hostilities took place, and my husband, who was thoroughly worn out, was able, for the first time in a long while, to lie down upon a bed. In order that his rest might not be in the least disturbed, I had a good bed made up for him in a little room; while I, with my children and both my maids, laid down in a little parlor close by. But about one o'clock in the night, someone came and asked to speak to him. It was with the greatest reluctance that I found myself obliged to awaken him. I observed that the message did not please him, as he immediately sent the man back to head-quarters, and laid himself down again considerably out of humor. Soon after this, General Burgoyne requested the

On the evening of October 10th, Captain Munro was told by a ranking British officer to escape while he could. In response, the boat captain paid his men and quietly departed for the safety of Canada.[189] Afterwards, Ensign Daniel Fraser was left in command of the bateaux company.

On October 14, 1777, with his army surrounded at Saratoga, Burgoyne ordered all of his loyalist troops, including the drafts, to depart on their own for Canada.[190] Under the cover of darkness, Fraser led the remainder of his men out of Burgoyne's camp. Each man carried only two days provisions.[191] Once outside, Fraser's men were joined by loyalists from Peter's Corps. Together, the two groups fled northward.

On October 17, 1777, as the men walked single file towards Lake George, cannon fire could be heard coming from the direction of Saratoga. At that moment, the weary regular troops were marching out in front of

presence of all the generals and staff officers at a council-of-war, which was to be held early the next morning; in which he proposed to break the capitulation… It was, however, finally decided, that this was neither practicable nor advisable."

[189] Hugh Munro, *Munro to Haldimand, January 10, 1778.* Letter.

[190] "List of McAlpin's Men Paid by Ensign Donald Fraser", October 14, 1777. Note that "Donald" was a Gaelic nickname for "Daniel"

[191] Fraser, *Skulking* at 55.

the victorious rebels to stack their arms and colors. The cannon fire heard were victory salutes fired by Gate's artillery. As one loyalist sadly stated "it went to my heart to hear it, though I knew it was to be the case."[192]

Under the surrender terms Burgoyne accepted, Article 8 of the Saratoga Convention stipulated that all captured persons were British subjects rather than subjects of the Continental Congress. Thus, loyalist prisoners of war were permitted to return to Canada if they signed paroles agreeing not to participate in future hostilities against American forces. A lieutenant, two ensigns, one surgeon, four sergeants and thirty eight rank and file from McAlpin's Corps were identified under the Saratoga Convention as paroled prisoners of war.[193] These men and officers were

---

[192] John Peters, "A Narrative of John Peters, Lieutenant Colonel of the Queen's Loyal Rangers in Canada, drawn by himself in a Letter to a Friend in London" Toronto Globe, July 16, 1877. "The 31st in the Morning we proceeded to Fort George which was entirely reduced to Ashes; where in the Afternoon we fortunately met with a Boat which carried us to Diamond Island about five Miles up the Lake where lay a Detachment of British Troops. On our Arrival here it gave me unexpressible Pleasure to think myself at a happy Distance from those scenes of outrage, Tumult, and oppression, and to find myself secure." Richard Cartwright Jr. *A Journey to Canada, c. 1777*. Journal. From http://www.62ndregiment.org/A_Journey_to_Canada_by_Cartwright.pdf.
[193] "Present State of the Several Detachments of Royalists who Returned from Lieutenant General Burgoyne's Army to Canada after the Convention", May 1, 1778.

likely captured during the First Battle of Freeman's Farm, subsequent

foraging and bateaux expeditions or after Burgoyne's surrender.[194]

However, on the eve of Burgoyne's surrender, McAlpin was

ordered to carry out a very dangerous and near impossible task. The

general ordered remaining Native Americans and McAlpin's Corps to take

possession of the army's military chest and transport it back to Canada.

That evening, the corps slipped out of camp and rushed north towards Fort

Ticonderoga and the safety of its garrison.

At the time of Burgoyne's defeat, Ticonderoga was under the

command of Brigadier Henry Watson Powell. As loyalist refugees from

Saratoga and reinforcements under Barry St. Leger streamed into the fort,

---

[194]For a detailed description of *British* prisoners and camp follower following the surrender of Burgoyne, see the Letter of Hannah Winthrop, November, 1777. "Last Thursday, which was a very stormy day, a large number of British Troops came softly thro the Town via Watertown to Prospect hill, on Friday we heard the Hessians were to make a Procession in the same rout; we thot we should have nothing to do with them, but View them as they Passt. To be sure, the sight was truly astonishing, I never had the least Idea that the Creation produced such a sordid set of creatures in human Figure—poor, dirty, emaciated men, great numbers of women, who seemd to be the beasts of burthen, having a bushel basket on their back, by which they were bent double, the contents seemd to be Pots & kettles, various sorts of Furniture, children peeping thro the gridirons & other utensils, Some very young Infants who were born on the road; the women with bare feet, cloathd in dirty raggs such Effluvia filld the air while they were passing, had they not been smoking all the time, I should have been apprehensive of being contaminated by them."

the troops under the command of Powell swelled from seven hundred to almost two thousand men. Nevertheless, despite this augmentation, Powell elected to evacuate Ticonderoga.

On November 1, 1777, Powell ordered the loyalists at his post, including McAlpin's Corps, to be put to work destroying the fortification.[195] According to loyalist Richard Cartwright Jr. "it being determined upon to abandon this Garrison, the Work of Destruction was already beginning, in one Part was seen Heaps of Carriages in Flames, in another the Heavy Artillery destroyed, and all in the greatest Hurry to get what could be removed without much Difficulty removed on board the Vessels. However this was but the beginning and we did not stay to seen the conclusion of the Scene, which ended with [illegible crossed out word] setting the Forts and Houses in a Blaze, for having with some Difficulty procured a Boat and got our baggage round to the Fort."[196]

---

[195] "Weekly State of the Fortification", November 1, 1777.
[196] Cartwright, *A Journey to Canada*.

On November 8, 1777, Fort Ticonderoga was abandoned by its garrison.[197] Cartwright noted "we set out from Ti at Dusk in the Evening, leaving behind Mr. Dowland who did not attend, and that Night went three or four Miles up the Lake, landed on the West Side, made a First and slept very comfortable near it in our Tent."[198]

As the garrison retreated northward, McAlpin's was charged, not only with protecting the pay chest, but also with driving a herd of cattle towards Canada.[199] Upon reaching the Bouquet River, a company of rangers under the command of Captain Ebenezer Allen intercepted the column and a brutal skirmish erupted. When the battle ended, fifty of McAlpin's men were captured or left behind as casualties.[200] Nevertheless, the loyalist officer was able to push past the enemy and successfully reach Canada with the military chest.

---

[197] Powell, to his credit, was able to withdraw with most of his supplies and livestock intact.

[198] Ibid.

[199] Theodore Corbett, *No Turning Point: The Saratoga Campaign in Perspective*, (Oklahoma, 2012), 251.

[200] *New York Gazette and Weekly Mercury*, November 17, 1777.

Chapter Nine: "Loyalists in Great Distress"

In early 1778, McAlpin was promoted to major and was given the arduous task of overseeing the flood of refugees who poured into Canada following Burgoyne's defeat. For McAlpin this was a monumental task. British authorities controlling Canada were ill prepared for the arrival of thousands of men, women and children who Haldimand fittingly described as "loyalists in great distress."[201] The constant stream of incoming refugees shocked the sensibilities of even the most hardened British officer. As Barry St. Leger noted, a group of loyalists arrived at Niagara "almost naked . . . they had been so long hiding in the woods that they were almost famished . . . 50 more are on their way but so weak they can

---

[201] Frederick Haldimand, *Haldimand to Germain, October 14, 1778*. Letter. Estimates place the number of non-military loyalists in Canada following the defeat of Burgoyne at over one thousand men, women and children. By 1780, the number of loyalist refugees in Canada had grown to five thousand. By 1784, the number would increase to seven thousand.

scarcely crawl... they are a set of poor forlorn people. . .who cannot help themselves."[202] Another contingent consisted of five women, thirty-five children and had one pair of shoes amongst them. They had taken shelter along the Mohawk River and were growing potatoes and corn to survive.[203]

The British approach to providing assistance to loyalists in Canada was similar to governmental policies towards the poor in England. Male loyalists were strongly encouraged, if not coerced, to enlist in military service. If they refused, their families were often denied access to

---

[202] Barry St. Leger, *St. Leger to Matthews, September 19, 1781.* Letter.

[203] Elizabeth Bowman Spohn, *Elizabeth Bowman Spohn to Rev. Egerton Rycrson, July 23, 1861.* Letter. "My father, Peter Bowman, the eldest son at home, was only eleven years old. As the pillage was at night, he had neither coat nor shoes; he had to cut and draw his firewood half a mile on a hand-sleigh to keep his sick mother from freezing; this he did barefooted. The whole family would have perished had it not been for some friendly Indians that brought them provisions. One gave my father a blanket, coat and a pair of mocassins. A kind Squaw doctored my grandmother, but she suffered so much through want and anxiety that it was not until spring that she was able to do anything. She then took her children and went to the Mohawk River, where they planted corn and potatoes; and in the fall the commander of the British forces at Niagara, hearing of their destitute situation, sent a party with some Indians to bring them in. They brought in five families: the Nellises, Secords, Youngs, Bucks, and our own family (Bowman), five women and thirty-one children, and only one pair of shoes among them all. They arrived at Fort George on the 3rd of November, 1776; from there they were sent first to Montreal, and then to Quebec, where the Government took care of them-that is, gave them something to eat, and barracks to sleep in. My grandmother was exposed to cold and damp so much that she took the rheumatism and never recovered."

necessary public assistance. Meanwhile, incoming female loyalists were questioned to determine what trade or skills they possessed and then were dispatched to specific locations to seek employment. Destitute loyalists, including the sick, infirm, children, women and cripples, were assigned to refugee camps and placed on public assistance. However, "public assistance" in the 18th century differed greatly from modern practices. Under 18th century British policies, those on public assistance received only bare necessities at minimal costs. More importantly, those on assistance were expected to work in exchange for their assistance. At many refugee camps, women and children were expected to make "blanket coats, leggings at cheaper rates than the Canadians."[204] To keep expenses low, loyalist women and children were mustered once a month so they could be inspected and determine whether or not they still qualified for public assistance.[205]

Unfortunately, the efforts of the British government to provide asylum for the loyalists were often in vain and as the years progressed,

---

[204] *Regulations as to the Lodgings and Allowances for Loyalists*, March 6, 1782.
[205] Ibid.

existing difficulties were compounded with an ever greater influx of refugees. Housing was the greatest problem. On September 14, 1778, Frederick Haldimand's secretary Conrad Gugy complained about the lack of pine wood for necessary housing for the refugees.[206] By December and the onset of the Canadian winter, loyalist housing was still not complete.[207] On January 7, 1779, Haldimand demanded to know why officials assigned to the Machiche refugee camp had not yet built the sawmill needed for the construction of housing and military barracks.[208] British authorities even experienced difficulties establishing a schoolhouse for refugee children.[209]

Living quarters for loyalist refugees were cramped at best. In December 1778 one hundred and ninety six refugees at Machiche were assigned to living quarters in one of twelve buildings. The following year, over four hundred refugees were placed in one of only twenty-one

---

[206] Conrad Gugy, *Gugy to Haldimand, September 14, 1778*. Letter. Construction of the first set of barracks was not completed until November 8, 1778. Conrad Gugy, *Gugy to Haldimand, November 8, 1778*. Letter

[207] Conrad Gugy, *Gugy to Haldimand, December 20, 1778*. Letter

[208] Frederick Haldimand, *Haldimand to Gugy, January 7, 1779*. Letter.

[209] Conrad Gugy, *Gugy to Haldimand, March 6, 1779*. Letter; *Gugy to Haldimand, March 14, 1779*.

buildings. Historical documentation suggests these structures were only eighteen by forty feet in size.[210]

British officials struggled to supply the loyalists with provisions, candles and blankets.[211] By 1783, over three thousand loyalists were in need of basic clothing, including over three thousand pairs of stockings and shoes and sixteen thousand yards of linen and wool.[212] The following year, British officials warned that several refugees had died "owing as they think for the want of provisions and clothing."[213]

Food supplies and cooking equipment were exceedingly difficult to procure as more loyalists arrived in Canada. Fresh meat was continuously

---

[210] *List of Loyalists and Their Families lodged at Machicheat This Date*, December 2, 1778; Conrad Gugy, *Gugy to Haldimand, November 16, 1778.* Letter.

[211] *Gugy to Haldimand, October 30, 1778; Gugy to Haldimand, November 8, 1778; Gugy to Haldimand, November 16, 1778.*

[212] *Estimate of Clothing Required to Clothe the Above Numbered of Refugees, Agreeable to the Proportions Heretofore Granted*, 1783. Great Britain, British Library Additional Manuscripts No. 21826, folio 103. That same year loyalists at Sorel were supplied with "360 yards of linen cloth, 149 yards of wollen cloth, 73 blankets, 110 pairs of stockings, 106 pairs of shoes and 10 pairs of short leggings and mitts." Haldimand to (?), December, 1783. It should be noted there were over 600 loyalists in and around Sorel at the time of this issuance.

[213] Stephen Delancey, *Stephen Delancey to Robert Matthews, April 26 and May 4, 1784.* Letters.

scarce[214] and full rations often withheld.[215] In correspondence with his superiors, Gugy warned that the children at the Machiche refugee camp were severely malnourished and many mothers were depriving themselves of their own food in an effort to keep their children alive.[216] To alleviate this problem, loyalists were encouraged to grow or secure their own food. To assist in this venture, Mr. Gugy established a pasture for fifty cows and a garden for growing vegetables.[217] Unfortunately, the efforts failed miserably.[218]

The treatment of black loyalists during the American Revolution, including those in Canada, was especially problematic. British authorities

---

[214] Gugy made no less than two requests in November, 1778 for provisions of fresh beef for the loyalists at Machiche. *Gugy to Haldimand November 8, 1778 and November 16, 1778.*

[215] Robert Matthews, *Robert Matthews to Abraham Cuyler, November 18, 1782.* Letter. To complicate matters, in 1778, the refugees at Machiche were only issued twenty-four kettles and eight frying pans to prepare their food. *Gugy to Haldimand, November 16, 1778.*

[216] John Ross, *Major Ross to Sir John Johnson, September 11, 1780.* Letter. Daniel McAlpin would also complain about the state of loyalist children and families under his care. "All are in a state of distress . . . and are in urgent need of help."

[217] *Haldimand to Germain, October 15, 1778.*

[218] By 1780, over two hundred and sixty-two men, three hundred and eight women and seven hundred and ninety eight children at various refugee camps outside of Montreal alone were wholly dependent upon public assistance in the form of food supplies from the government. McKinnon, *While the Women,* 107-110; HP 21, 826.

encouraged slaves to profess their loyalty to the Crown in exchange for freedom. However, once escaped slaves reached British lines, they often found that promise unfulfilled. Some were taken prisoner and either claimed as property by their captors or sold for profit. Likewise, British officials consistently maintained that former slaves of loyalists had to be returned to their masters. Many loyalist officers protested the treatment of black loyalists and expressed their "sensible feelings [we] have for [our fellow Creatures".[219] One officer, Daniel Claus, asserted that African-American soldiers were often of great help to scouting and raiding parties. He then noted sadly that sixteen blacks he had brought in as recruits "for their loyalty ... now are rendered Slaves in Montreal."[220]

---

[219] William Parker, *William Parker to Haldimand, February 16, 1782*. Letter; Robert Mathews, *Mathews to Sir John Johnson, October 6, 1783*. Letter; Robert Mathews, *Mathews to Captain Leake, December 16 1781*. Letter.

[220] Daniel Claus, *Claus to Haldimand, December 9, 1779*. Letter.

144

Black Loyalist Woodcutter by Captain William Booth

To contain the impact of refugees on the Quebec Province, British authorities restricted loyalists and refused to let them travel outside of their respective camps.[221]   As a result, refugees quickly discovered that they could not supplement their meager supplies with trips to neighboring towns and villages. Services, including laundry, were subject to price fixing under the threat of being removed from public assistance.[222]

---

[221] *Gugy to Haldimand, October 30, 1778.*

[222] "The loyalist women receiving rations are to wash for the non-commissioned officers and men of the volunteers at four coppers a shirt and in proportion for other things." Frederick Haldimand, *Haldimand to Lieutenant French, July 14, 1780.* Letter.

Likewise, requests to sell goods, including alcohol, to complement their meager living conditions were summarily denied.[223]

From the refugee perspective, most were horrified at their living conditions, lack of provisions and severe restriction of movement. As one group of loyalists opined, "we shall not be able to overcome the Seveir and approaching hard winter ... [in] a Strange and Disolate place where [we] can get nothing to Work to earne a Penney for the Support of Each Other . . . much more the Bigger part of us Without one shilling in our pockets and not a Shew on our feet."[224] Another loyalist complained that his refugee camp was a "drowned bog without water."[225] Many refugees accused Gershom French, a loyalist in charge of supplies at Machiche, of abusing loyalists and diverting basic materials to himself.[226]

An even greater concern amongst refugees was the presence of camp fever which was quickly spreading through the refugee sites. Other

---

[223] *Gugy to Haldimand, November 32, 1778.*

[224] *Petition by His Majesty's Faithful Subjects Emigrated Under the Conduct of Captain Michael Grass from New York to This Place*, Sorel, September 29, 1783.

[225] *Gugy to Haldimand, October 2, 1778; Petition to Mr. Gugy,* November 12, 1778.

[226] *Complaint by John Peters*, January 20, 1780.

deadly diseases present at the camps included malaria, small pox and pneumonia.[227] Loyalists chafed at the government's downplay of camp conditions and the assertion that their complaints were "frivolous".[228] According to a letter from Gugy to Stephen DeLancy, inspector of the loyalist camps, he was "well aware of the uniform discontent of the Loyalists . . . the discontent . . . is excited by a few ill-disposed persons. . . . the sickness they complain of has been common throughout the province, and should have lessened rather than increased the consumption of provisions."[229]

As years passed and loyalists continued to be confined inside refugee camps, families and individuals collapsed under the psychological burden. Long term absences of loyalist men on military missions only exacerbated the situation. There was one recorded incident of infanticide at Carleton Island where a mother killed her newborn.[230] Marriages crumbled, alcoholism rose and emotional breakdowns became

[227] *Ross to Haldimand, November 25, 1782.*
[228] *Gugy to Haldimand, October 2, 1778.*
[229] *Gugy to DeLancy, April 29, 1780.*
[230] Ibid.

commonplace.[231] In short, death and tragedy surrounded the loyalists in Canada.

From the British perspective, Haldimand became exasperated with the refugees and described them as "a number of useless Consumers of Provisions."[232] He summarized the distaste British authorities had for the unappreciative refugees when he told a prominent loyalist "His Excellency is anxious to do everything in his power for the Loyalists, but if what he can do does not come up to the expectation of him and those he represents, His Excellency gives the fullest permission to them to seek redress in such manner as they shall think best."[233] In short, loyalists were forced to choose between accepting life in refugee camps or fend for themselves.

---

[231] W. Stewart Wallace, *The United Empire Loyalists: A Chronicle of the Great Migration, Volume 13.* (EBook, 2004), http://www.gutenberg.org/files/11977/11977.txt. See also *Tuttle to Matthews, July 11, 1781; MacLean to Matthews, November 24, 1779; St. Leger to Haldimand, November 16, 1782; Claus to Haldimand, June 14, 1784.* There are period accounts of several "insane loyalists" being sent from refugee camps to hospitals in Quebec.

[232] *Haldimand to Johnson 23 May 1780; Haldimand to Powell, 15 March 1780.*

[233] http://www.canadiangenealogy.net/chronicles/loyalists_quebec.htm HYPERLINK "http://www.canadiangenealogy.net/chronicles/loyalists_quebec.htm"

Chapter Ten: "They Have Sacrificed All They Had for Their Loyalty"

When McAlpin's Corps of American Volunteers returned to Canada, the organization was a decimated shell of what it had been months earlier. Worse, Captain Munro was once again making overtures to remove his bateaux company from the Corps. Yet McAlpin was prepared for the upstart Munro. When Munro refused for a second time to muster his men with McAlpin's Corps, he was removed from his command, taken off the military payroll and relegated to the task of supervising the building of a bridge in Berthier.[234] McAlpin replaced Munro with one of his own men.

Over the next two and a half years, Munro would try in vain to regain his command and seek the return of his men to him. His final

---

Munro to Haldimand, January 10, 1778 and September 12, 1780.

attempt occurred on December 7, 1780, six months after McAlpin's death. In a letter to Robert Matthews, Munro outlined his grievances against the loyalist commander and demanded reinstatement as senior captain in the corps. He went even further and proposed that the corps be divided into two military units and a share of men be assigned to him. The requests were forwarded to Major John Nairne, superintendent of loyalist forces in Canada, who summarily denied the requests.[235]

While McAlpin was fending off Hugh Munro, the major still faced the daunting task of overseeing several loyalist corps and rebuilding his own corps of volunteers stationed at Sorel.[236] Complicating matters were the Jessup brothers. Still reeling from losing a portion of their recruits to

---

[235] *Munro to Matthews, December 7, 1780.*

[236] "Quebec 17th May 1779 . . . Sir . . . As I Shall probably have Occasion this Summer to Employ You, &Your Regiment, upon Some active and important Service, I am anxious that you Should now be employed, in preparing them for this purpose, and in order to prevent other Business from interfering with this Principal Object, I have thought proper to appoint Captain McALPIN to have the Command and Direction of the Several Corps of Loyalists, including both those who are paid, and those who are not,and in a few Days Captain McALPIN will Wait upon you to Receive all Instructions, Lists, or any other Papers in Your Possession, which May assist him in arranging these Irregular Corps-and I request, you will give Captain McALPIN every private Information in Your Power relative to this part of the Service. It will be necessary that you Send Orders to the Heads of all Corps, and to the Individuals who belongs to no particular Body, that they immediately put themselves under the Command and Direction of Captain McALPIN. I am with great Regard Sir, Your most Obedient humble Servant Fred: HALDIMAND."

McAlpin in August of 1777, both brothers repeatedly complained to authorities that their corps was significantly understaffed and recruits stolen by McAlpin needed to be returned. On one occasion, Ebenezer Jessup wrote to Brigadier General John Powell and demanded almost seventy men recruited be returned to his corps.[237] The request was quickly denied. Almost a month later, Neil Robertson complained to Sir John Johnson that the Jessup brothers tried to persuade him to return sixty-eight men currently enlisted with McAlpin's Corps. Robertson also rebuffed the demand, correctly pointing out that of the sixty-eight men requested, "25 of whom are among the rebels, 22 dead or deserted, the other 21 belong to Major Daniel McAlpin's corps."[238]

McAlpin recognized his unit was in danger and could be broken up and dispersed amongst the other loyalist units stationed in Canada. McAlpin quickly petitioned Haldimand, arguing "that your Excellency will be good enough to support them in their different stations, as they

---

[237] Ebenezer Jessup, *Ebenezer Jessup to Powell, July 26, 1780.* Letter.
[238] Niel Robertson, *Robertson to Johnson, August 6, 1780.* Letter.

have sacrificed all they had for their loyalty."[239] Haldimand agreed and

McAlpin's Corps remained intact. However, McAlpin would spend the

rest of his military career trying to bring his unit back up to its pre-

Saratoga strength. Unfortunately, it would be a goal that would never be

reached.[240]

A West View of Sorel, ca 1784 National Archives of Canada/C-002005 Artist: James Peachey

Throughout 1778 and most of 1779, McAlpin's Corps remained in

Sorel, a town located in southwestern Quebec Province. When not

---

[239] *McAlpin to Haldimand, November 18, 1778.*

[240] It appears Haldimand attempted to supplement the ranks of McAlpin's Corps with regular troops. For example, on August 30, 1778, General Haldimand ordered a company of the 34th Regiment of Foot not only to join McAlpin's Corps, but to mix itself into the ranks and assist the Corps with its duties. The company remained attached to McAlpin's Corps until December 18, 1778. By January 1, 1779, the 34th was back serving in the ranks of McAlpin's Corps. It appears the unit remained with McAlpin's until September, 1779.

engaged in garrison duty, McAlpin's men were employed in the construction and repair of earthworks around the town.[241] The roads leading to and from Sorel were frequently in poor condition. Coupled with Carleton's belief that most, if not all, of the provincial forces in Canada would be reassigned to the main American theater, resupply and soldier's pay was often intentionally withheld and thus difficult to obtain.[242]

As a result, McAlpin struggled to ensure his men were properly armed and equipped. Recognizing that his men were armed with a mix of old French military muskets, fowlers and commercial trade guns, McAlpin argued "I need not explain to His Excellency the figure an old grey-headed fellow will make at the head of a parcel of raw, undisciplined people with bad arms . . . I hope the General will be good enough to prevent me from appearing in this mortifying situation by ordering good arms to be

---

[241] Daniel McAlpin, *McAlpin to Matthews, July 29, 1779.* Letter.
[242] Daniel McAlpin, *An effective list of all Loyalists in Canada receiving provisions. Report of Captain Daniel McAlpin, July 1, 1779*; *McAlpin to Haldimand, May 4, 1779.*

delivered to us."[243] It appears McAlpin did make some progress and did receive some "good arms" in 1778. Nevertheless, as late as August 3, 1778, McAlpin still reported a "return of arms and accouterments wanting to compleat Captain McAlpin's Corps of Volunteers . . . 35 firelocks, 35 bayonets, 35 belts and frogs, 35 cartridge boxes."[244]

Major McAlpin also repeatedly begged British authorities to properly clothe his troops. Despite his best efforts, his men would not receive new uniforms until November, 1778. Worse, this would be the only identified clothing the American Volunteers would receive over the next two years.[245] It is unclear whether these coats were the highly unpopular blue coats faced white that Jessup's Corps received in December, 1778.[246] If so, the men and officers of McAlpin's Corps

---

[243] Great Britain, British Library, Additional Manuscripts, No. 21821, folios 29-30. See also *McAlpin to Matthews, July 29, 1779*.
[244] Great Britain, Public Record Office, War Office, Class 28, Volume 10, folio 44.
[245] *McAlpin to Haldimand, June 8, 1780*.
[246] Jim Kochan theorizes that these blue faced white coats were "prize" clothing taken from seized rebel stores in Canada or Ticonderoga or from captured rebel supply ships.

followed the example of Jessup's Corps and elected to wear blanket coats instead of the coats often worn by their New England enemies.[247]

Life at Sorel was often difficult. Besides a lack of supplies, shelter was almost non-existent. As Sir. John Johnson correctly noted in correspondence to Haldimand regarding McAlpin's and other corps, "I have not mentioned Tents, or Camp Equipage, tho they [are] wanting for

---

[247] "With all Respect and due difference we the subscribing Officers of the Loyalists beg leave to represent to
Your Excellency, that the Cloathing in Store at this Garrison being Blue faced with White, the same as
the Uniform of many Regiments of our Enemies, we are apprehensive that should we be sent on service
with this Cloathing, many fatal accidents might happen, from mistakes of Indians and our own Scouting Parties, as was actually the case several times last Campaign. We are aware that to expect this Cloathing should be totally laid aside, for such reasons, after the great expense the Crown has been at, must be deemed unreasonable; our wishes only are that Your Excellency will Order us, Red Clothing, as along as any remains in Store, and that the Blue may be made use of the last. Lieut Colonel St. Leger has been pleased at our request to suffer us to draw only half Mounting, for the present, the Blanket Coats we have purchased for the Men by his directions, supplying the place of the Coats, untill Your Excellency will be pleased to decide for us; and whatever that decision may be we shall be entirely satisfied – The Transporting the Cloathing at this Season, we are sensible will be attended with some Expense to Government, which we do not wish to burthen it with; but should Your Excellency Order us the Red Clothing we will chearfully defray the Expense of Carriage." *Jessup et al to Haldimand, December 2, 1778.* Great Britain, British Library, Additional Manuscripts, No. 21821, folio 5.

the whole Regiment – but should your Excellency think them Necessary, I shall immediately forward them."[248]

Worse yet, the volunteers of McAlpin's Corps often found themselves at odds with civilian refugees living in Sorel. Competition for limited supplies, including fresh food and clothing, proved to be a source of constant irritation. On more than one occasion, Major McAlpin described incidents of large groups of loyalist refugees engaged in fights with his soldiers.[249]

Likewise, intoxication was an ongoing problem. In one instance during a visit to Sorel by the famed Robert Rogers and his recruiter named Pritchard, almost all of the loyalist troops assigned to Sorel got drunk, abandoned their posts and abused their officers. Naturally, Major McAlpin was horrified at the 'Pritchard Affair" and demanded that Rogers be prohibited from returning to Sorel.[250]

---

[248] *Johnson to Haldimand, May 20, 1779.*

[249] For an example of a soldier-civilian dispute, see *McAlpin to Matthews, January 16, 1780.*

[250] "St. Ours 26th Decr. 1779, Sir I was favoured with your letter of the 16th. The moment I received it I wrote to Captain Sherwood, and he informs me that the men inlisted by Mr. Prichard has been Musterd and received pay and Cloathing since the year

An Opportunity for Revenge: The Raid on Johnstown

It 1780, McAlpin's Corps of American Volunteers returned to New

York. For these loyalists, participation in the 1780 military raids was

more than opportunity to get away from the boredom of garrison duty.

1777, and there is not the least doubt of the Truth of it. I have got my man back, the others stands as they were inlisted by Prichard. Mr. Prichard is a Loyalist from New England that received Seven Pounds pr. Muster Subsistance from Govrt. The men that he enlisted were Employed in the Engineer Department at St. Johns. Mr. Prichard told them if they were not Sworn by a Justice of the peace they Could not be Deem'd Soldiers and would inlist them in spite of any officer of the Loyalist[s.] This affair had like to be serious. The Loyalists Employed in the Engineers Departmt. at Sorel got Drunk with those Recruiting parties, neglected their work and talk'd to the Engineer and to their own officers as independent of them. They were promised Commissions and Large pay by Major Rogers. This is not the only Complaint against Major Rogers proceeding in this affair. A man of the name of Betties whom I sent out from Genl. Burgoyns Camp to bring in some Loyalists that were Engaged for me is lately come to this province with ten men. When they arrived at St. Johns both he and his men Declared they were Engaged for me and Betties Drew upon me for money for their support at St. Johns which Draft I have answered. As Soon as they arrived at Montreal Brigadier Genl. McLeans party and Major Rogers got about them, Major Rogers got hold of Betties Desired him to go to his Taylor and fit himself with a Suit of Superfine Scarlet. The Brigadier as I am told, sent for Beatties and told him that Rogers Taylor could not fit as well as his Taylor and insisted upon his taking a Suit from him. The men are still at Montreal and I don't know which of the Gentlemen will gain the prize. Betties was musterd and received some pay from me in Genl. Burgoynes Camp, and I hope His Excellency Genl. Haldimand will be good Enough to allow my Taylor to fit Mr. Betties and his men with Cloaths. I have reason to think that my Taylor will fit them much better than either of the other two Gentlemen. I have reason to expect Justice done me and I have not the least doubt about it. I don't wish to be a prey to Every adventurer that Sets up to raise a Corps. I have the honor to be with Great Respect Sir Your most obedient Humble Servant Danl: McAlpin Brigadr. Genl. Powell" Great Britain, British Library, Additional Manuscripts, No. 21821, folios 37-38.

157

Instead, these raids represented an opportunity of revenge for the failures of Saratoga.

In March, 1780, Ensign Walter Sutherland of the King's Royal Regiment of New York returned from a scout to Johnstown, New York. In his report to Haldimand, Sutherland disclosed that New York rebels intended to force all military age men, including loyalists, into units stationed along the Canadian border. Those who refused would be arrested, their homes destroyed and their property confiscated. Alarmed, Haldimand ordered Sir John Johnson to organize a relief force with the intent to evacuate all military age loyalist men and their families from the Johnstown area.[251]

In preparation for the raid, Haldimand ordered three separate detachments consisting of thirty four men and two officers from the 29th, 34th and 53rd Regiments and one detachment composed of an officer and twenty men from the Hesse Hanau Jaegers to assemble at Ile-aux-Noix. One hundred and sixty-one men from the King's Royal Regiment were

---

[251] Gavin Watt, *The Burning of the Valleys*, (Toronto, 1997), 75.

also recruited for the mission, as were fifty men recruited from McAlpin's Corps of American Volunteers, Peter's Queen's Loyal Rangers and Jessup's King's Loyal Americans. On April 13, 1780, the loyalist detachments of the raiding party were ordered to also assemble at Ile-aux-Noix. Upon arrival, the entire raiding party, over five hundred and twenty-eight men in total, were placed under the command of Sir John Johnson and Captain Thomas Scott of the 53rd Regiment.[252]

The troops were transported by water from Ile-aux-Noix down Lake Champlain to Crown Point. Once on land, the soldiers travelled to the south-west, skirting around Schroon Lake. On May 21, 1780, the raiders attacked Kingsborough Patent, located north of Johnstown, and rescued one hundred forty three loyalists, including women and children, and thirty slaves.[253] Johnson then led his troops into Johnstown, burned several buildings, rescued dozens more loyalists and captured twenty-

---

[252] Ibid at 77-78.

[253] Ibid. With Sir John Johnson's blessing, several of the raiders broke away from the main body, sought out several officers of Third Regiment, Tryon County Militia and killed them.

seven rebels. Afterwards, the raiders burned one hundred and twenty

barns, mills and houses located in a four mile arc south of the township.[254]

New York authorities rushed to stop the loyalists and dispatched

over eight hundred Continental troops and militia to intercept Johnson and

his men. A second force of nine hundred rebels was raised in the

Hampshire Grants and ordered west towards Johnstown. Over the next

four days, the raiders, their prisoners and loyalist refugees were doggedly

pursued by the Americans and forced to continuously change direction as

they withdrew towards Crown Point. However, Johnson successfully

reached the ruined fort and escaped by water just as two thousand rebel

troops and militia arrived at the shoreline of Lake Champlain.[255]

Fortunately, the rebels were unable to pursue and were forced to watch

helplessly as their prey escaped north to Canada.

---

[254] Ibid at 79.
[255] Ibid.

The Death of Daniel McAlpin

In the weeks following the Raid on Johnstown, Daniel McAlpin's health deteriorated drastically. Despite the efforts of his physicians, the major never recovered from the long term exposure to the elements while he hid from rebel patrols in 1777. On July 22, 1780, McAlpin succumbed to his illnesses and passed away. The news of his death travelled quickly and by July 25, 1780, Haldimand was informed of the loss of his major.

McAlpin's passing was a tremendous blow, emotionally and financially, to his family. For the next two years Mrs. McAlpin and her children lingered in Canada. On March 15, 1781, Mary McAlpin personally appealed to Haldimand for help. According to the general, Mrs. McAlpin pleaded that as a result of outstanding debts accrued by Major McAlpin "only the sum of £633 17s 3d remains for the support of herself and her two daughters."[256] Surprisingly, it was the Jessup brothers who were among the first to step forward and donate funds to support the

---

[256] *Petition to Haldimand, March 15, 1781.* A partial smudge appears between the numbers 6 and 3. However, upon closer examination, it appears Mary McAlpin is claiming she has only £633 remaining.

McAlpins. Unfortunately, the monies raised were only sufficient for the short term and a scandal involving her only son exacerbated her financial situation.[257]

By 1782, the McAlpins' financial situation was desperate and as a result, they were forced to sail for England. While in London, Mary McAlpin repeatedly petitioned British authorities for £6000 in compensation for personal and real property lost at the hands of New York rebels during the American Revolution. By 1788, her petition still remained unanswered and she was forced to survive on a small pension. Mary McAlpin and her children never returned to America.[258]

McAlpin's death also had a significant impact on his corps. Recognizing that their protector and sponsor could no longer shield them from the Jessup Brothers or Hugh Munro, the men of the American Volunteers wrote a petition to Haldimand on August 24, 1780. In their letter, the men informed the governor that they considered themselves

---

[257] See Appendix F

[258] Fraser, *Skulking* at 61.

"freed by his death" and requested that Haldimand dissolve the unit.[259]

Haldimand quickly rejected the petition. The fate of McAlpin's Corps of American Volunteers was quickly sealed and in less than eighteen months, the corps would cease to exist.

Major John Nairne of the 1st Battalion, 84th Royal Highland Emigrants was given command of the American Volunteers, as well as the other loyalist corps previously supervised by McAlpin. Recognizing the relative weakness of numbers of each of these corps, the major ordered the various units merged into a single corps that would become known as the "Corps of Royalists".[260] Each provincial unit composed a single military company within the corps. By November, 1780, Nairne turned command of the American Volunteers over to Captain Gideon Adams of Connecticut.

---

[259] *Petition to Haldimand, August 24, 1780.*
[260] By October 10, 1780, the numerical strength of the American Volunteers was 8 commissioned officers and 82 effective rank and files.

Major John Nairne

Like McAlpin, Nairne quickly recognized that the men under his command needed to be properly clothed and equipped. According to Ebenezer Jessup "Major Nairn told me that he had sixty suits of clothing which he should distribute to the men [at] Yemeska Post and to the recruits for the Late McAlpin's Corps . . . the severity of the weather makes me ask for [additional] cloathing."[261]

---

[261] Ebenezer Jessup, *Ebenezer Jessup to Captain Matthews, December 1, 1780.* Letter.

164

To ascertain the gravity of the situation, the major ordered "all the officers and Men belonging To the Several Corps of Royalists Quartered in this Parish to assemble at his quarters on thirsday 12th Instant...What ever arms and accutrments the officers and Men are Possessed of are to be Brought along with them that all Deficiences May appear and Proper applications Shall be made for Every Necessary Equipment for those who are ancious to Serve as Soldiers During the war..."[262] According to one loyalist officer, the inspection revealed that many of the loyalist soldiers were still "in great want of Provisions; and was distressed for everything having wore out all their Shoes, Mockosins, Trowsers, Leggings, &c..."[263]

Following the inspection of his men, Nairne rushed to secure proper clothing for his troops. On January 4, 1781, he instructed "Mr. Titus Simons . . . to over look the Taylors belonging to the Corps of Royalists and Take Perticolar Care that They Shall on No Pretences Do

[262] Jessup's Orderly Books, Regimental Orders, December 9, 1780.
[263] John Munro, *Captain John Munro to Captain Richard Lernoult, November 20, 1780.* Letter.

Any Other Work Till the Clothing . . . is finished."[264] By April 1, 1781,

Nairne had not only secured enough clothing for all of his troops,

including green uniform coats faced red, but had accumulated a surplus of

100 additional uniforms and enough material for 30 more, 370 leggings

and 756 stockings.[265] However, due to logistical issues that often plagued

the British army, not all of the uniforms were issued to the Corps of

Loyalists. As late as January 2, 1782, Edward Jessup begged "the

Commander in Chief That the men in the Corps of Royalists are in great

want of Cloathing and that I Beg His Excellancy will pleas to give orders

for their being issued."[266]

---

[264] Jessup's Orderly Books, Regimental Orders, January 4, 1781.

[265] General Return of Stores and Batteaux in the Quarter Master Generals Department in Canada – Head Quarters Quebec, April 1, 1781. A review of the returns suggest that the soldiers under Nairne's command should have also been issued Russian drill breeches or gaitored trousers, linen shirts, shoes, blanket coats and "rolers".

[266] *Edward Jessup to Captain Matthews, January 2, 1782.*

Chapter Eleven: The October Raids[267]

On August 24, 1780, Governor Haldimand proposed a series of coordinated raids into New York to "destroy the enemy's supplies from the late plentiful harvest and to give His Majesty's loyal subjects an opportunity of retiring to this province."[268] The projected raids also had a secondary objective of demonstrating to the residents of the Hampshire Grants, who had been making questionable overtures to Haldimand about switching sides, the true strength of the British forces stationed in Canada.

The planned raids into New York would move in multiple columns down the Mohawk, Lower Champlain and Hudson River Valleys and

---

[267] The following section describes McAlpin's Corps role in Major Christopher Carleton's raid during the month of October 1780. McAlpin's participation in this raid is based upon a confession by James Van Driesen. On October 25, 1780, Van Driesen asserted to his captors that that McAlpin's Corps was part of Carleton's forces. It should be noted Gavin Watt questions the credibility of the claim and believes that Van Driesen was enlisted with King's Rangers, not McAlpin's Corps of American Volunteers..
[268] *Haldimand to Johnson, August 24, 1780.*

would be carried out by troops and Native allies under the command of Major Christopher Carleton of the 29th Regiment of Foot, Sir John Johnson and Captain John Munro of the King's Royal Regiment of New York and Lieutenant Richard Houghton of the 53rd Regiment of Foot.

The attack of the Lower Champlain and Hudson River Valleys fell to Major Carleton. On September 27, 1780, over 950 men from regular and loyalist units assembled at St. John's. According to loyalist James Van Driesen, McAlpin's Corps was one of the units drafted for the mission.[269] On September 28th, the troops sailed to Ile-aux-Noix and by October 2nd, the expedition had reached Valcour Island. The next day, Carleton's men set up camp at Split Rock, where they remained until October 6th.

That evening, Carleton's men travelled south past Crown Point to the ruins of Fort Ticonderoga[270]. On October 8th, Carleton departed from the fort and advanced towards Fort Ann via bateaux. Two days later, as

---

[269] Victor Hugo Paltsits, *Minutes of the Commissioners for detecting and defeating Conspiracies in the State of New York, Albany County Sessions, 1778-1781*, (Albany, 1909).
[270] Ticonderoga was abandoned by the British in November, 1777.

the British forces descended on the simple wooden block house, the garrison surrendered without firing a shot. Seventy-five officers and enlisted men were taken prisoner and the fort was quickly burned to the ground.[271] The same day, Carleton continued south towards Fort Edward. En route, he burned every farm that he encountered, with the exception of two owned by loyalist yeomen. Once at the North Hudson River, the raiders turned west towards Fort George. Upon arrival at the Kingsbury District, Carleton torched the town.

The next day, the soldiers advanced on Fort George. The commander of the fort, Captain John Chipman, quickly learned of Carleton's approach. Believing that the enemy was a small war party, he dispatched fifty soldiers under the command of Captain Thomas Sill to intercept Carleton. In turn, Carleton dispatched a large flanking party of Indians, King's Rangers, McAlpin's Corps and the 34th Regiment of Foot.[272] The American party was ambushed at Bloody Pond and quickly

---

[271] It is unclear whether the prisoners were sent back to South Bay or to Fort Ticonderoga.
[272] Ibid.

surrounded. In the heavy combat that followed, twenty seven American soldiers were killed, two were wounded and eight captured. Only thirteen men escaped. Carleton's men sustained no casualties.

Carleton displayed most of his troops in full view of Fort George on Gage's Height. Captain Chipman ordered American artillery pieces to open fire on the enemy. However, after three ineffective shots, the captain quickly realized he was in an untenable position and started negotiations with Carleton to surrender. Within hours the garrison capitulated and on October 12th, Fort George was burned to the ground.

Believing his mission was complete, Carleton turned north and marched back towards Fort Ticonderoga. By October 25th, Carleton and his men were well on their way back to Canada. However, that same day the major received orders to return to New York and harass the rebels once again. By October 30th, Carleton was atop Mount Independence. For the next two weeks, Carleton engaged in a "cat and mouse" game with rebel forces active in the "Narrows", an area of Lake Champlain between Mount Independence and Fort Ticonderoga.

On November 12th, Carleton withdrew his forces and sailed for Canada. By November 14th, he arrived at St. John's.

The October Raids were a complete success. Not only had Carleton destroyed two forts, captured dozens of enemy soldiers, burned several towns and kept rebel forces in check, but he had done so with minimal casualties. At the conclusion of the raids, only two men were killed, three were wounded and two deserted. James Van Driesen was the only loss attributable to McAlpin's Corps of American Volunteers. Shortly after the engagement at Bloody Pond, Van Driesen deserted and fled southeast towards Ballstown. Upon arrival, he alerted the local militia of Carleton's activities. For his information, Van Driesen was rewarded with imprisonment, trial and a death sentence. However, Governor Clinton intervened on Van Driesen's behalf and on February 27, 1781, he was released on bail.[273]

Following the October Raids, McAlpin's Corps returned to garrison life at Sorel. For most of 1781, the soldiers watched as an

---

[273] Ibid.

unending stream of loyalist refugees poured into the garrison town. In turn, many loyalists came to terms with their current status and concluded that they would never return to New York or New England. As a result, many of these men attempted to carve out some semblance of a new life at Sorel. On February 8, 1781, Haldimand reported that residents and soldiers alike cleared out wood lots around Sorel and started construction of a windmill.[274] By July, saw mill and brick kilns were constructed and fully operational.[275] That November, bakeries were approved by Haldimand.[276]

The Loyal Rangers

As the Revolutionary War raged in Virginia, Haldimand began to secretly make overtures to the representatives of Vermont, formerly the Hampshire Grants, to abandon the revolutionary cause and declare loyalty to England. On October 14th, Haldimand ordered Barry St. Leger to deliver a proclamation to Vermont seeking reunification with England. At

---

[274] Frederick Haldimand, *Haldimand to Twiss, February 8, 1781.* Letter.
[275] *Haldimand to Twiss, July 1, 1781.*
[276] *Haldimand to Twiss, November 22, 1781.*

the same time, the general was ordered to conduct a diversionary action in support of John Ross, who had launched a raid into the New York interior via Fort Oswego. Per Haldimand, St. Leger was expected to lead troops to the upper end of Lake Champlain and establish a base of operation at Crown Point. Although St. Leger was ordered not to engage in hostilities from Crown Point unless attacked, the general was expected to dispatch raiding parties towards Lake George. Within a week, St. Leger had assembled over 900 regular, German, Native American and loyalist troops. Among those soldiers and under the command of Captain Edward Jessup were the volunteers of McAlpin's Corps.

On October 17, 1781, St. Leger's force departed Sorel and sailed for Ile la Motte. Two days later, the small army arrived at Crown Point and then pressed southward towards Fort Ticonderoga. Once there, the group secured the Lake George landing and carried their boats overland from Lake Champlain to Lake George.

On October 24, 1781, two hundred and five loyalists, sixty light infantry and forty Jaegers under the command of Captain Jessup assembled at the landing with fourteen day's rations and fifty rounds each. At nine o'clock in the evening, the detachment "sailed most peaceably three miles, landed on a small island, built many fires and without taking the least precaution against surprise, slept undisturbed and passed the night thus." [277] After two nights on the island, Jessup's detachment set sail once again.

Jessup and his men stopped at three separate islands and lit large signal fires on each. This action, coupled with a brief firefight with a rebel patrol, alarmed the countryside. Surprisingly, Jessup's detachment continued operations on Lake George unchecked. According to St. Leger, the expedition focused on intelligence gathering between Stillwater and Saratoga and establishing contact with local Mohawks. By November 1st, the expedition returned to Fort Ticonderoga and by November 4th, withdrew towards Crown Point. By November 13th, the expedition passed Ile aux Noix and retired into Canada.

---

[277] Gavin Watt, *A Dirty Trifling Piece of Business: Volume 1 The Revolutionary War as Waged from Canada in 1781,* (Toronto, 2006), 384.

While the men of McAlpin's Corps were returning home, General Haldimand finally concluded that the various loyalist units left over from the Burgoyne campaign and still under his command had utterly failed in their recruiting efforts. On November 12, 1781, Haldimand released his *Proposal for Forming the Several Corps of Loyalists*. In his order, Haldimand instructed that Jessup's, Peter's and McAlpin's Corps be amalgamated into a single battalion designated the Loyal Rangers. Edward Jessup, Ebenezer's brother, was promoted to major and placed in command of the unit. In support of his decision, Haldimand asserted "His Excellency . . . robust constitution, his personal activity, merit and experience having served last war, are circumstances which render him a fit person to command the above mentioned corps." The men and officers of McAlpin's Corps were dispersed amongst the ten companies.[278]

As with Nairne and McAlpin, Major Jessup also struggled to clothe his troops. A little more than a month after assuming command, Jessup complained "the men in the Corps of Royalists are in great want of

---

[278] "Proposal for Forming the Several Corps of Loyalists", November 12, 1781.

Cloathing and that I Beg His Excellancy will pleas to give orders for their being issued of the green Cloaths as we understand there is a sufficient Quantity of that sort to Cloath the whole Corps . . . Capt Sherwood tells us that his Coat is approved of as a pattern for our uniform which we shall Immetate but shall need some green Cloath for facings (as the Present facings are Red) I thought it would be but Little Expence if any Rat eaten or Damaged Coats Should be in the Store."[279] Ten days later, Jessup ordered "The Captains and Commanding Officers of Companys are to Deliver without delay to the Acting Adjutant an Exact Return of their non Commissioned Officers Drummers and Private Men in their respective Company for whosoever it will be Necessary at Present to give Cloathing."[280] By February 14th, the commander was still submitting requests for additional clothing.[281] On February 21, 1782, Jessup was able to report that only one hundred and seventy-four green regimental coats faced red had been issued to his men.

---

[279] *Edward Jessup to Captain Matthews, January 2, 1782.*
[280] Jessup's Orderly Book, January 12, 1782.
[281] *Jessup to Matthews, February 14, 1782.*

Following the formation of the Loyal Rangers, the battalion was transferred from Sorel to Verchere, Yamaska and Dutchman's Point.[282] The Loyal Rangers spent most of its time garrisoning the blockhouses at these three posts. The unit was constantly utilized for long range security patrols as well. As Jessup reported "we are obliged to keep up a Constant round of Scouts . . . and that I have already been obliged to furnish several of the men . . . and must furnish Several More Soon or not get any Scouting from them."[283]

---

[282] Three lieutenants, nine sergeants and two hundred and six soldiers were stationed at Verchere. Two ensigns, four sergeants and fifty-seven soldiers occupied Dutchman's Point. One lieutenant, five sergeants, one drummer and seventy-seven soldiers garrisoned Yamaska.

[283] Ibid.

Chapter Twelve: Ernestown

When peace was declared in 1783, the most pressing issue for
Haldimand was what to do with the thousands of loyalist refugees who
occupied the Quebec Province. Many were without clothing and few had
received sufficient supplies.[284] The general contemplated a forced
removal of the refugees to parts unknown. However, by July 1783 many
loyalist officers, including Edward Jessup, proposed the settlement of land
south-west of the Quebec Province. The suggestion was quickly adopted
and land grants were issued to loyalist soldiers and refugees alike.

On September 5, 1783, Jessup reported to British authorities that
many of his rangers were interested in settling tracts of land north of
Ottowa, known initially as the "Second Town" and renamed in 1784 as

---

[284] *Jessup to Matthews, April 12, 1783.*

Ernestown in honor of King George's fifth son Prince Ernest Augustus.[285]

Six days later, a plan of settlement was drafted for Jessup[286] and called for

settlements to be established for each company from the Loyal Rangers.[287]

On December 11, 1783, the Loyal Rangers were formally

disbanded and its soldiers and families were permitted to depart for the

grants of lands issued to them.

Loyalist Encampment at Johnson, Ontario 1784 by James Peachy

By May 1784 Governor Frederick Haldimand ordered those

refugees who still remained in the Quebec province to vacate their

respective camps and proceed to Sorel. Upon arrival, the loyalists were

[285] *Jessup to Matthews, September 5, 1783.* The settlement area of Ernestown also included the area of modern day Bath, Ontario, Canada
[286] Ibid.
[287] *Jessup to Matthews, January 29, 1784.*

mustered and provisioned for the voyage to the new settlements on the

Canadian frontier. Each man and boy over ten was issued a coat,

waistcoat, breeches, hat, shirt, blanket, shoes and shoe soles, leggings, and

stockings. Women and girls over ten received two yards of woolen cloth,

four yards of linen, one pair of stockings, a blanket, and shoe soles, while

small children qualified for one yard of woolen cloth, two yards of linen,

stockings, and shoe soles. One blanket was provided for every two

children and and groups of five people were expected to share a single tent

and one cooking kettle.[288] Farm tools, including grain sickles, were also

issued as well.

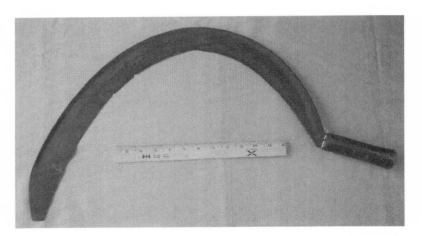

---

[288] John Barnes, *Captain John Barnes to Haldimand, September 24, 1784.* Letter.

Surviving Grain Sickle issued to Loyalists by the British Government in 1783.

Once supplied, loyalists were ushered to Lachine for transportation

to the west. Refugees were loaded onto flat-bottomed boats that ranged in

size from twenty-five to forty feet long and could accommodate four to

five families and their belongings at the same time. Once the bateaux

were loaded, the vessels were assembled into squadrons of twelve and set

out, being powered variously by oars, poles, or sails. The trip was slow

and trying. Rapids forced the passengers and their belongings out of the

batteaux, which had to be dragged and pulled with ropes through the

churning waters. Winds, rapidly changing weather patterns and

mosquitoes made the trip more difficult. At night the passengers had to

sleep in makeshift tents or brush huts pitched near open fires used for

cooking.[289]

Upon arrival at designated settlements, loyalists literally had to

rebuild their lives. Life on the Canadian frontier was difficult at best.

Money was scarce and markets for supplies were almost non-existent. By

---

[289] Anne Powell, *Description of a Journey from Montreal to Detroit in 1789*, (1789).

June 1784, Jessup reported that development of the frontier settlements were behind schedule.[290]

Despite the challenges, loyalist Justus Sherwood asserted "that the people have got on their farms, are universally pleased, are emulating each other so that every lot in the front of the three townships and many of those in the back townships are improved and the country bears a very promising appearance."[291] Months later, Jessup informed government officials "the settlement is going on much better than he expected from the lateness of the season and the reduction of provisions. The allowance made by His Excellency made a great change and the people act with resolution and spirit, but if the allowance is discontinued they will be much distressed."[292]

By October 1784, the development of Ernestown had progressed to the point Jessup reported the discovery of iron ore and proposed the

---

[290] *Jessup to Matthews, June 24, 1784.*
[291] Justus Sherwood, *Sherwood to Matthews, July 23, 1784.* Letter.
[292] *Jessup to Matthews, September 8, 1784.*

construction of iron works as well as saw and corn mills.[293] By 1785, the settlement had expanded to include over one thousand men, women and children.

In the years before the War of 1812 Ernestown continued to grow, partly because of its location at the mouth of the Bay of Quinte and partly because of its role as the supplier of foodstuffs to Kingston. Several decades later the historian William Canniff asserted that town rivaled even Kingston and pointed to its rapid increase of inhabitants, strong trade operations, the establishment of several ship building yards and the presence of several gentlemen of refinement and education.

As Ernestown entered the second decade of the 19th Century, the threat of another armed conflict with the United States loomed. Fearful that American troops would invade Canada and drive loyalists from their home, the residents of Ernestown joined neighboring towns in drafting *From the Inhabitants of Upper Canada to the People of the American States*. Although the primary focus of the document is the retelling of the

---

[293] *Jessup to Matthews, October 5, 1784.*

brutality and violence the average loyalist refugee faced during the American Revolution and their willingness to defend their homes, the final sentence correctly surmised the changed attitude of the loyalists towards their American counterpart. Gone was the hope of returning to their lives and homes as they were before the Revolution. Instead, the residents of Ernestown and other townships simply declared "we want nothing of yours".[294]

---

[294] *Kingston Gazette*, October 31, 1812.

Appendix A

<u>Muster Roll of Jessup's Corps at Point Clair, January 24, 1777</u>

Captain Edward Jessup's Company

Rank	Name
Lieutenant	Peter Drummond
Ensigns	William Lamson
	William Snyder
Sergeant	John Buel
Corporal	Martin Kelly
Privates	James ???
	Ames More
	Thomas Barns
	John McDonald
	John Siley
	Daniel Robertson
	John McFarson
	John Perrey
	Ebenezer King

	John Stiles
	Robert Dickson
	Thomas Barton
	Simon Snider Zachariah Snider
	Samuel Perry
	Christopher Bennett
	George Tuttle
	Thomas Loveless
	Silas Hamblin
	Alexander Munro
	Daniel Camron
	Archibald Nicholson
	Samuel Camron
	John Maloy
	Gespor More
	Peter McGregor
	Angus Canedy
	Peter McCallum

	Abraham Crozier
	William Forbes

Captain Jonathan Jones' Company

Rank	Name
Lieutenant	Peter McLaren
Ensign	Neil Robertson
Surgeon's Mate	Solomon Jones
Sergeant	Francis Scott
Corporal	John Dickson
Privates	Carath Brisbon
	Jeremiah Myers
	Nicholas Amey
	Martinus Stover
	Jonas Amey
	Peter Lane
	Armstrong Williams
	Matthias Rose
	Patrick Carrigan
	John Sanders

	John Scott
	Peter Maybee
	David Miller
	Adam Earhart

	Daniel Rose
	William Rogers
	John Williams

Captain Ebenezer Jessup's Company

Rank	Name
Lieutenant	Joseph Jessup
	David Jones
Ensign	George Thomas Bulsan
Sergeant	Peter Carrigan
Corporal	John German
Privates	Jeremiah Storms
	Simon Earhart

	John McDonie
	Ralph Spooner
	Abraham Brown
	Adam Waggoner
	Peter Carpenter
	Angus McCornuch
	John Gamble
	John Sea
	Duncan Carrigan
	Simon Shereman
	James Sea
	Jeremiah Snider
	Richard Wood
	James Wilson
	Duncan Campbell
	Hiramus Lea

Appendix B

List of Loyalists Refugees Living at Machiche 1779

Name	Number of Children	Husband's Occupation or Military Status
Mrs. Holt	no children	-
John Holt	an able young man	-
Mrs. McLaren	no children	(husband Lieut)
Mrs. Naughton	3 children	(husband Ensign)
Mrs. Munro	1 child	(husband Ensign)
Mrs. Froom	2 children	(husband artificer)
Mrs. Shorey	3 children	(husband soldier in R.H. Emigrants)
Mrs. Dixon	2 children	(Jessup's Corps)
Mrs. Hamelin	2 children	(Jessup's Corps)
Mrs. Perry	8 children	(Lieut)
Mrs. Adams	4 children	(husband Lieut)
Mrs. Lovelace	7 children	(husband Ensign)
Mrs. England	3 children	(husband Cap't McAlpin's Corps)

Peter Gilchrist	-	(Labourer)
William Fergueson	-	(Labourer)
Mrs. Fergueson	4 children	(Labourer)
Mrs. Johnson	3 children	(husband in Adam's Corps)
Mrs. Lee	2 children	(husband in Jessup's Corps)
Mrs. Stover	2 children	(husband in Jessup's Corps)
Mrs. Beatts	1 child	(husband in Adam's Corps)
Mrs. Amey	2 children	(husband in Jessup's Corps)
Mrs. N. Amey	3 children	(husband in Jessup's Corps)
Mrs. Snyder	4 children	(husband Ens. in Jessup's)
Mrs. Hawley	-	-
Mr. Hawley	0 children	(Cooper)
Isaac Briscow	3 children	(Adam's)
Mrs. Seevot	1 child	(Peter's Corps)
Mrs. Henderson	1 child	(Peter's Corps)
Mrs. Grey	2 children	(husband in Peter's)

Mrs. Moshier	1 child	(husband in Peter's)
Mrs. French	5 children	(Lieut. in Peter's Corps)
Mrs. Hard (Hurd)	2 children	(husband in Peter's Corps)
Mrs. Hard (Hurd)	1 child	(husband in Peter's Corps)
Mrs. Reddenback	4 children	(Corp'l in McAlpin's)
Mrs. Wragg	6 children	(husband prisoner with rebels)
Josiah Cass	-	(Schoolmaster)
Mrs. Cass	6 children	-
Mrs. Robertson	3 children	(husband Private in Adam's)
Mrs. Strider	0 children	(husband soldier in Sir John's Reg.)
Mrs. Defrige	6 children	(a widow)
Mrs. Benedict	1 child	(Adam's Handmaid)
Mrs. Hawley	5 children	(husband in Adam's Corps (Lieut)
Mrs. Timy	4 children	(husband in Adam's Corps (Lieut)

Mrs. Perry	3 children	(husband in Peter's Corps)
Mrs. Sherman	5 children	(husband in Jessup's Corps)
Jeremiah Hilliker	-	(no corps)
Mrs. Hilliker	0 children	-
Mrs. Brown	2 children	(husband in Jessup's Corps)
Mrs. Beech	3 children	(husband Sgt. in Peter's Corps)
Mrs. Hopson	0 children	(husband Ensign)
Mrs. Brooks	1 child	(husband Corporal in Peter's Corps)
Mrs. Anderson	1 child	(husband Cap't In Sir John's Reg.)
Mrs. Lampson	2 children	(husband an Ensign)
Mrs. Campbell	0 children	(husband Ensign in Cap't McAlpin's Corps)
Mr. & Mrs. Nicholas Brown	0 children	(silversmith... no corps)

Appendix C

<u>Statistical Breakdown of Forty-One 1777 Recruits from McAlpin's Corps of American Volunteers as Drawn from a 1783 Muster Roll of the Loyal Rangers</u>

Ethnic Makeup

A. 12 Men from Scotland (30%)
B. 6 Men from Ireland (15%)
C. 1 Man from Germany (2%)
D. 1 Man from England (2%)
E. 21 Men from America (51%)

Military Rank

A. 2 Captains
B. 1 Lieutenant
C. 5 sergeants
D. 1 Corporal
E. 32 Privates

Age Distribution

A. Oldest: 2 men 61 years of age
B. Youngest: 1 man 19 years of age
C. Average: 35 years of age
D. Breakdown of ages:
      1. 12 - 19: 1

2. 20 - 29: 14
3. 30 - 39: 14
4. 40 - 49: 4
5. 50 - 59: 2
6. 60 - 69: 3
7. Unknown: 3

Height Distribution

A. Tallest: 2 men at six feet
B. Shortest: 2 men at five feet four inches
C. Average: five feet seven inches
D. Breakdown of height:
    1. 5'4": 2
    2. 5'5": 2
    3. 5'6": 6
    4. 5'7": 8
    5. 5'8": 8
    6. 5'9": 3
    7. 5'10": 6
    8. 5'11: 1
    9. 6': 2
    10. Unknown: 3

Company Distribution from McAlpin's Corps into the Loyal Rangers

A. Captain Jonathan Jones' Company: 1 Corporal, 8 privates
B. Major Edward Jessup's Company: 2 Privates
C. Captain John Peter's Company (Invalids): 1 Sergeant, 6 privates
D. Captain William Fraser's Company: 1 Captain, 1 sergeant, 5 privates
E. Captain John Jones' Company: 3 Privates

F. Captain Peter Drummond's Company: 1 Captain, 1 Sergeant, 9 privates
G. Captain Justus Sherwood's Company: 1 sergeant
H. Captain Thomas Fraser's Company: 1 sergeant

Appendix D

Return of the Officers of the Corps of Loyal Rangers
Commanded by Major E. Jessup[295]

Name	Place of Origin or Birth	Length of Service and/or Remarks
Major Edward Jessup	Connecticut	7 years Served the last war a volunteer in the Militia, and the campaign 1759, a company of Provincials, which he raised at his own expense; has been for some years a Justice of the Peace for the County of Albany, where he possessed a considerable property, until deprived of it by the late rebellion.
Captain Ebenezer Jessup	Connecticut	7 years

---

[295] J.F. Pringle, Lunenburgh or the Old Eastern District, (Cornwall, 1890).

		Was a Justice of the Peace for the County of Albany, in the Province of New York, where he possessed a considerable property, until he was deprived of it by the rebellion. He began to raise a corps and served as Lieut.-Colonel in the campaign under Lieut.-General Burgoyne in 1777; from that year he received pay as a captain, and owing to infirmities when the corps was again formed in the year 1781, he was continued as captain and the command given to Major Jessup.
Captain John Peters	Connecticut	7 years Was a Justice of the Peace for the County of Gloucester, on Connecticut River, where he possessed property. He began to raise a corps, and served under Lieut. General Burgoyne in the campaign of

		1777 as Lieut.-Colonel, but from that year to November, 1781, he was paid as captain, and from the impossibility of his filling a corps and his own infirmities he was continued as captain in ye loyal Rangers.
Captain Justus Sherwood	Connecticut	7 years

Was a farmer of property in what is now called the New Vermont State, and deprived of it by the late rebellion, through which he has been both active and zealous in opposing it. |
| Captain Jonathan Jones | Connecticut | 7 years

Was a Justice of the Peace for the County of Albany, in the Province of New York, where he had a farm, mills, and other property, of which he was deprived by the late rebellion. |
| Captain William Fraser | Scotland | 6 ½ years |

		A farmer of property in the Province of New York, of which he was deprived by the late rebellion.
Captain John Jones	Connecticut	6 ½ years
		A farmer of property in the Province of New York, which he was deprived of by the late rebellion.
Captain Peter Drummond	Scotland	7 years
		A farmer of property in the Province of New York, of which he was deprived by the late rebellion.
Captain John W. Meyers	New York	6 ½ years
		A farmer in the Province of New York, of which with other property to a considerable amount lost by the rebellion.
Captain Thomas Fraser	Scotland	6 ½ years
		A farmer of property in the Province of New York, lost by the rebellion.
Lieut. Guisbert Sharp	New York	6 ½ years

		A wealthy farmer in that Province, lost by the rebellion.
Lieut. Henry Simmonds	New York	6 ½ years A farmer of property in that Province, lost by the rebellion.
Lieut. David Jones	Connecticut	7 years A farmer of property in the Province of New York, lost by the rebellion.
Lieut. James Parrot	Boston	7 years A farmer of property in the Province of New York, lost by the rebellion.
Lieut. Alex'r Campbell	New York	6 ½ years A wealthy farmer of some considerable property in that Province, lost by the rebellion.
Lieut. David McFall	Ireland	7 years Was many years a sergeant in the 26th Regiment, where he served with credit.

Lieut. John Dulmage	Ireland	7 years A farmer of property in the Province of New York.
Lieut. Gershom French	Connecticut	7 years A young man of some property who had commenced business as a merchant just at the beginning of the trouble in America.
Lieut. Gideon Adams	Connecticut	7 years A young farmer of property.

Lieut. John Ritter	N. Yk.	6 ½ years A farmer of property in that Province.
Lieut. James Robins	Old England	6 ½ years A country merchant in the Province of New York.
Lieut. Edward Jessup	N. Yk.	6 ¼ years Major Jessup's son, and entirely dependent on his father.
Ensign John Dusenbury	N. Yk.	6 ½ years

		A wealthy farmer's son in that Province.
Ensign John Peters	Connecticut	6 ½ years Son of Col. Peters, and dependent on his father.
Ensign Elijah Bottom	Connecticut	6 ½ years A farmer's son in that Province.
Ensign Thomas Sherwood	Connecticut	4 ½ years A farmer in the Province of New York.
Ensign Thomas Mann	N. Yk.	6 ½ years Son of a gentleman farmer in that Province.
Ensign Harmonius Best	N. Yk.	6 ½ years A farmer of property in that Province.
Ensign William Lawson	Connecticut	7 years A farmer in the Province of New York.
Ensign Conrad Best	N. Yk.	6 years A farmer in that Province.

Adjt. Matthew Thompson	Ireland	2 years A sergeant-major in the 31st Regiment, where He had served Line many years as a non-commissioned officer with credit.
Quarter Master John Fergnson	Ireland	1 year A sergeant-major in the 29th Regiment, where he had served many years as a non-commissioned officer with credit.
Surgeon George Smyth	Ireland	2 ½ years A physician in the Province of New York.
Mate Solomon Jones	Connecticut	7 years Student of his profession in Albany, in the Proy. of New York.

Appendix E

The Ensign James McAlpin Affair

James McAlpin was the only son of New York loyalists Daniel and Mary McAlpin. Born in 1765, McAlpin resided with his parents and sisters, Isabella and Mary, in Stillwater, New York. However, in May of 1774, his father purchased approximately one thousand acres of land located on the west side of Saratoga Lake (in the present Town of Malta) and immediately proceeded to improve upon it. The McAlpin family moved to their new home in 1775. By 1776, the family was already building a second home on the property.[296]

At the outbreak of the American Revolution, the McAlpin family was firmly in support of the British Crown. This was due to land and investment interests the family held in the Hampshire Grants. As a result, the family was subjected to a series of escalating hostile acts at the hands

---

[296] The homes were timber log planked and floored. The houses were valued at £100 and £200 respectively. A value of £1 Sterling per acre unimproved and £2.10 Sterling improved was placed on the land. By the summer of 1777 there were at least 170 acres in high cultivation. Captain McAlpin had 20-25 servants in constant employ on his farm.

of local rebel organizations known as the "Tory Committees". In February, 1777, after rejecting repeated overtures to join the American cause, a mob appeared at the McAlpin home. James' father was forced to flee without his family and hide in nearby woods for over two weeks. When local officials discovered that Daniel McAlpin was recruiting loyalist soldiers and attempting to send them to Canada, a bounty of $100 was set for his capture of McAlpin.[297] Captain Tyrannis Collins of the Albany County Militia was ordered to arrest McAlpin and "carry [those] who were supposed to be disaffected to the country, as prisoners to Albany."[298]

Realizing he had been exposed, Daniel McAlpin was forced to flee to safety without his family.[299] McAlpin remained in hiding until Burgoyne's army arrived at Fort Edward in August, 1777.

---

[297] "Proceedings April 17, 1777". *Minutes of the Albany Committee of Correspondence.* From Internet Archive, *Minutes of the Albany Committee of Correspondence, 1775-1778, Vol. 1.* From https://archive.org/stream/MinutesOfTheAlbanyCommitteeOfCorrespondence1775-1778Vol1/MinutesOfTheAlbanyCommitteeOfCorrespondence1775-1778Vol1_djvu.txt.
[298] J. Fraser, *Skulking for the King*, (Ontario: Boston Mills Press, 1985), 35.
[299] Ibid.

Shortly after his escape, Daniel McAlpin's property was seized and his wife and family were arrested. Mary McAlpin described her family's treatment at the hands of the rebels in vivid language. "From the day her husband left to the day she was forced from her home the Captain's house was never without parties of the Rebels present. They lived at their discretion and sometimes in very large numbers. They destroyed what they could not consume. Shortly after the capture of the fleeing loyalists a group of armed Rebels with blackened faces broke into the McAlpin's dwelling house. They threatened Mary and her children with violence and menace of instant death. They confined them to the kitchen while they stripped every valuable from the home. A few days after this, by an order of the Albany Committee, a detachment of Rebel Forces came and seized upon the remainder of McAlpin's estate both real and personal."[300] Mary McAlpin and her children were taken to an unheated hut located in

---

[300] *American Loyalists, Transcripts of the Manuscript Books and Papers of the Commission of Enquiry into the Losses and Services of the American Loyalist*, IV, 284. From Robert Woodward Barnwell, Jr., "George Harland Hartle'ys Claim for Losses as a Loyalist," *The South Carolina Historical and Genealogical Magazine*, 51, no. 1 (1950), 43-47, 54, 51-62.

Stillwater and locked inside "without fire, table, chairs or any other convenience."[301]

Hoping that the hardship would eventually break Mrs. McAlpin and induce her to beg her husband to honorably surrender, the rebels kept Mary and her children in captivity for several weeks. Mary McAlpin refused to comply and instead responded her husband "had already established his honour by a faithful service to his King and country."[302] Enraged, rebels seized Mary and her oldest daughter and "carted" both of them through Albany. According to one witness "Mrs. McAlpin was brought down to Albany in a very scandalous manner so much that the Americans themselves cried out about it."[303] A second account stated "when Mrs. McAlpin was brought from the hut to Albany as a prisoner

---

[301] Ibid. On May 27, 1777 General Gates condemned the actions of local militiamen who raided the McAlpin home. However, Gates did little to prevent McAlpin's property from being sold to support the American war effort.
[302] William Smith, *Memoirs of William Smith, May 12, 1777*. Edited by William H.W. Sabine (New York, 1956).
[303] Great Britain Audit Office Records, Volume 21, reel number B-1159.

with her daughter . . . they neither of them had a rag of cloaths to shift themselves."[304]

At some point during the Burgoyne invasion, the McAlpin family was released from rebel custody and joined their father. While Mary and her daughters fled to Canada, James remained behind and joined his father's unit, The American Volunteers. In October, 1777 at the mere age of twelve, James McAlpin was appointed to the rank of ensign.[305] It is unknown what combat or service experience, if any, James had in the final days or aftermath of the Burgoyne Campaign. Nevertheless, James remained on the American Volunteers muster rolls as an ensign for the next three years.

On July 22, 1780, Daniel McAlpin succumbed to a long illness and passed away. In the aftermath of his death, many loyalist officers directed their attention towards James. It is possible that while alive, James' father either failed to ensure his son received proper training as an officer or

---

[304] Ibid.

[305] *Muster Roll of the Corps of Royalists Commanded by the Late Daniel McAlpin, Verchere, July 14, 1781.* WO28/4/279.

covered his son's gross incompetence. Major John Nairne, who succeeded

Daniel McAlpin as commander of the American Volunteers, suggested

that the young officer was completely out of his element. "[His] time is

quite lost while he stays here & I beg you may contrive as much business

for him as possible, only (as he is young) that he may not be exposed to

much fatigue, or to be lost in the woods."[306] As a result, Nairne advised

Lieutenant William Fraser that McAlpin would be transferred out of the

American Volunteers to a loyalist post at Vereche "to be employed on

some Military Duty, and also in Writing and accompting."[307] General

Frederick Haldimand approved of the order but noted inexperienced the

boy was.[308] The general expressed hope that "by the time [McAlpin]

knows a little of his duty he will succeed to a lieutenancy."[309]

On December 1, 1780, James McAlpin was commissioned a

second lieutenant in the 1st Battalion of the King's Royal Regiment. He

was posted to the prison island of Coteau du Lac and was placed under the

---

[306] Nairne to Fraser, May 26, 1781, research conducted by Todd Braisted.
[307] Ibid.
[308] Haldimand to Johnson, July 27, 1780, HP 21,789, f. 84
[309] Ibid.

command of Captain Joseph Anderson. McAlpin oversaw thirty soldiers, a block house and an unknown number of American prisoners of war.[310]

While stationed at Coteau du Lac, McAlpin discovered that several of the American prisoners under his care were involved in the plundering of his family home and abuse of his mother and sisters.[311] In February, 1782, an intoxicated McAlpin had the offending prisoners "strung up" and tortured. Upon sober reflection, the young officer realized his mistake and begged forgiveness from the prisoners.

Nevertheless, American prisoners under McAlpin's care continued to be treated quite poorly. As Author J. Fraser suggests in his work *Skulking for the King*, McAlpin tortured his prisoners, ignored deteriorating health conditions and deprived them of basic necessities.

---

[310] Gray to Twiss, October 20, 1781, HP 21, 789, f. 271; De Speth to Haldimand, October 16, 1781, HP 21, 789, f. 271.
[311] Gavin Watt, *I Am Heartily Ashamed: Volume II - The Revolutionary War's Final Campaign as Waged from Canada in 1782,* (Dundum, 2010) p. 205.

In the early summer of 1782, five American prisoners escaped from Coteau du Lac. On June 10th, two of the escapees were apprehended by German soldiers. The poor physical and mental condition of the Americans was immediately apparent. When interviewed, the prisoners described to German officers how McAlpin deprived them of soap, proper food, clothing, shoes, tobacco and other provisions.

Brigadier General Ernst Ludwig Wilhelm De Speth immediately reported the incident to Haldimand.[312] In turn, Major Gray and four captains were dispatched to Coteau du Lac to investigate the claims. Both soldiers and prisoners reported that McAlpin was often intoxicated and treated the Americans poorly. The ensign was quickly arrested.

On July 15, 1782, Haldimand noted in his general orders that McAlpin was to be subject to a court martial due to the "most barbarous and inhumane treatment of prisoners."[313] During the hearing, American prisoners testified how food provided to them was crawling with vermin,

---

[312] De Speth to Haldimand, June 10, 1782, HP 21,790, f. 10.
[313] General Orders of Haldimand, Quebec, July 15, 1782, HP 21,743, ff. 195, 197.

blankets and straw were intentionally withheld and many were deprived of the simple necessity of water. As one prisoner recounted "some of the men became so dry and thirsty they were attacked with the raising of the blood."[314] Another described that because of the poor treatment at the hands of McAlpin, he would likely be a "cripple for the remainder of his life."[315]

The court quickly ruled that Ensign McAlpin was "guilty of the crime laid to his charge in breach of the twenty-third article of the fifteenth section of the articles of war."[316] He was immediately sentenced "to be Dismst his Majestyes Service."[317]

James McAlpin's military career ended at the age of seventeen.

Why McAlpin abused the prisoners under his charge is somewhat unknown. One potential motivating factor was his family's treatment at the hands of the Americans back in New York. Another possible cause

---

[314] Fraser, *Skulking* at 60-61; New York Genealogical & Biographical Society, *Asa Fitch Papers,* nos. 261, 275 and 500.
[315] Ibid.
[316] General Orders of Haldimand, Quebec, July 15, 1782, HP 21,743, ff. 195, 197.
[317] Ibid.

was his father's failing health and ultimate death, both of which were likely caused by Daniel McAlpin being forced to hide in caves and the woods for months on end. Given his young age, McAlpin also could have been easily influenced by the soldiers under his command. Finally, a lack of proper training and guidance from his superiors likely contributed to his actions.

Shortly after his conviction, James McAlpin, as well as his four sisters and mother, left Montreal and sailed for England. None of the McAlpins ever returned to America. Instead, the family took up residence in London. In her Loyalist Petition claim, Mary McAlpin makes little to no reference of her son or his military career. Instead, she focuses on the hardships of her husband, daughters and herself.

It appears that James never submitted his own claim to the English government. What became of the disgraced officer after his arrival in England remains a mystery.

Did You Enjoy this Book?

If so, I would be extremely grateful if you would <u>leave a review on Amazon.</u>

A review will help other potential readers to decide whether this book could be of use to them.

Your assistance is greatly appreciated. Again, you can post your review on Amazon.

Test Readers Wanted!

If you would like to join my launch team and receive all of my future publications (nonfiction and fiction) for free, please email me at mcalpin77@gmail.com.

What's involved:

As a launch team member, you will get access to a free reviewer copy (pdf) one to two weeks in advance of each book launch. You will have to read the book within a given time frame, provide feedback and leave a review on Amazon as soon as the book goes live.

You pick which books you would like to review.

Interested?

Then email me at mcalpin77@gmail.com!

Other Books by Alexander R. Cain

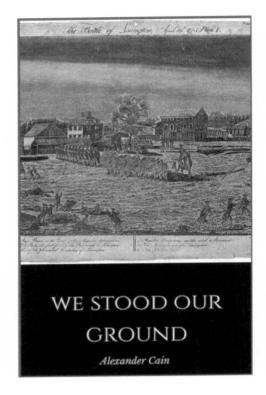

We Stood Our Ground